GOODNIGHT, SWEETHEART

A STORY OF FAITH, HOPE, AND LOVE

ALAN JOHNSTON

SONCOAST PUBLISHING

CONTENTS

INTRODUCTION

Roberta Flack had a hit song titled *The First Time Ever I Saw You.* That wonderful song opens with the words, *"The first time ever I saw your face I thought the sun rose in your eyes...."* I first laid eyes on Judy Gale Abercrombie on a bitterly cold, January 1985, evening at a meeting in a Chattanooga, Tennessee Methodist church. We had our first official date in March 1985, and on that first date we attended a Baptist Church meeting in Nashville, Tennessee. By May 1985 I was hopelessly in love with this beautiful, charming and vivacious woman. My reaction to Judy was described by one of my closest friends as "struck." He was right, I was struck! Struck indeed! Every time I saw her, I was struck again, and again, and again.

Judy and I married on May 2, 1987. Just before Christmas of that same year a movie, starring Cher and Nicolas Cage, premiered in New York City. That movie was *Moonstruck*, which went on to be highly acclaimed and the winner of many awards. Judy and I watched that movie so many times I lost count. Every time we watched, and I mean every time, I would kiss her and remind her that the title, *Moonstruck*, was a definition of me from the first time that I saw her.

The last time I watched that movie was Christmas 2018. Judy had died on October 6, 2018, following a fifteen- year battle with Alzheimer's Disease. I simply could not resist the urge to watch the movie, at least one more time. She and I had always found plenty to laugh about in the movie – but I readily admit that I found that those parts we found so funny still brought a smile, but now the smile was accompanied by warm, wet streaks of tears down my face.

One movie critic once said that the theme of *Moonstruck* is love and pain. In an elaboration on that thought he said, "…It's about love and pain: Falling in love, maintaining or losing love…broken hearts…recovering from the pain of lost love."

I have no doubt that for as long as her cognitive abilities allowed, Judy knew that I loved her with a relentless passion, and that I would have willingly, without hesitation, traded places with her. I too, knew that I had never known the kind of love that Judy had shown and shared with me. And, in words and actions, she made sure I knew that. Loving Judy led to a broken heart and much pain. Yet, in the words of the Apostle Paul, "love never ends." He also said, "faith, hope and love abide (stable, fixed, continuing for a long time), these three, but the greatest of these is love." In Roberta's song are found these words, *"I knew our joy would fill the earth and last 'till the end of time…."*

It is my hope that this love story will enable all who read it to come to the realization that even in tragic, life altering circumstances, it is possible to move forward, to recover from great loss – all while abiding in faith, hope and love. Time as we experience and express it ended on that October day in 2018. Yet, I know that in the realm of spiritual reality neither time nor love ended for Judy and me. Like King David, who upon the loss of a young child, said, *"But now he is dead…. I shall go to him, but he cannot return to me."* My faith and hope have secured for me the full conviction that love never dies. Ours is an endless love.

Following Judy's death, I found myself simply going through the motions of an everyday existence. An even emptier house, no routine that involved seeing Judy, work, study, writing and even church was just a blur, with one day bleeding into the next. About six weeks after Judy's death an old friend sent me a package. The package contained a wooden picture frame, and that frame contained a page from an old hymn book. I remember, as a kid, standing in church and singing that hymn. I had not thought of that hymn in a long, long time. But now, it was balm for my aching heart.

> Face to face with Christ my Savior,
> Face to face what will it be,
> When with rapture I behold Him,
> Jesus Christ who died for me?
>
> Only faintly now I see Him,
> With the darkling veil between;
> But a blessed day is coming,
> When His glory shall be seen.
>
> What rejoicing in His presence
> When are banished grief and pain;
> When the crooked ways are straightened
> And dark things shall be plain.
>
> Face to face! O blissful moment!
> Face to face to see and know;
> Face to face with my Redeemer,
> Jesus Christ who loves me so.
>
> Face to face I shall behold Him,
> Far beyond the starry sky;
> Face to face in all His glory,
> I shall see Him by and by.

Add to that the words of the Apostle Paul in 1 Corinthians 13:12, "*Now I know in part; then I shall know fully, even as I am fully known,*" and I can't wait. See you soon, Sweetheart!

Yes, faith, hope and love will carry us through any storm.

DEDICATION

With all the love that I have, and with utmost gratitude, I dedicate this book to

The Memory of Judy

Whose memory will linger until the day God calls me home. And we then see each other face to face once again.

"Meeting you was fate, becoming your friend was a choice, but falling in love with you, I had no control over." (W. Irving)

The Memory of Mother

It is very possible that only Jesus loved me more than my mother. Her remarkable love for Judy, demonstrated in so many ways, was a testimony of what resided in her heart. For me it was true, "life did not come with a manual, but thankfully it did come with Mother."

In Honor of Charlotte

"Just as lotions and fragrance gives sensual delight, a sweet friendship refreshes the soul." (Proverbs 27:9 MSG)

No one will ever doubt Charlotte's love for Judy, and Judy loved her back. I am forever grateful for the blessing of Charlotte in our lives.

OH WHAT A NIGHT

Blustery winter winds and a snow shower pushed me even more quickly that evening as I made my way across the parking lot and into the church. Then darting quickly into the fellowship hall for our meeting I was greeted by the familiar banter and chatter that filled the room every Monday evening. These people had become acquaintances of mine during the past month, and in reality, some of them had become a lifeline that I had been searching for for some time. I had arrived there on that first night I visited, more than a little embarrassed to even be there. We humans have a natural tendency to think no one's pain is as great as our own. No one could possibly understand my story. How does a thirty-five-year-old Baptist preacher even begin to explain the "why" of his presence? Of course, such thinking is completely unfounded and unnecessary, and that was soon proven to me. Each Monday this group gathered, and in some way, each of their stories had hints of my own story. Remember, we gathered in a church, not a bar, but this place was our version of the long running television show, *Cheers*. Each Monday night as I walked in it was as though a weight was lifted... and, yes, everyone knew my name.

PRETTY WOMAN WALKING DOWN THE STREET

Little had been different this evening. I can't even begin to remember who sat with me at dinner. We had some of the typical conversation you might expect from friends who did not see each other very often and rushed to bring everyone up to speed on our most recent week. We always had terrific desserts, so I am certain it was good; we had finished dessert, and the evening program had begun. Again, I don't recall what the program for that Monday evening was, only that for that evening we had a speaker. The room, as usual, was comfortably filled, and the speaker was into the presentation. I may or may not have been paying attention, but suddenly I was called to attention. Just beyond the speaker was a doorway, and now through that door walked the most stunning, gorgeous woman I had ever seen. Even from a distance I could see her dazzling, dancing black eyes. Her shoulders were draped in long wavy hair and as she strode into the room, I could not miss the color coordinated (very) high heels and her dress. I will never lose the image of her that night. The dress was somewhat of an eggshell color with lavender stripes. She oozed with confidence and her beauty was self-evident, if not in fact spell binding. Rather than shuffle through the crowded room she stopped along the front wall where a supply table was located. Brushing aside a few of the supplies she simply leaned back onto the table and remained there for the duration of the program. I am rather certain I never stopped looking her way. Wow! She was not more than ten feet from our table. Wow again! As the meeting ended, I leaned to the person seated to my right and quickly asked, as I nodded with my head toward her, "who is that woman?' I received a one- word answer, "Judy." In August 1964 Roy Orbison released a song that immediately soared to number one on all the charts. By October 1964 it had already been certified as a gold record. It was Orbison's greatest hit of his entire career. That song, was of course, *Pretty Woman."* The song expresses the absolute wonder of seeing such a marvelous creature with the word "mercy." Many who have known me for a long time know that my typical expression of wonder is, "my soul." I can assure that on that particular evening, having seen Judy for the first time, I said, "my soul."

That incredible song has other verses, but all I know is that night I drove home singing that song to the woman whose image would not leave my mind. I did not yet know it, but I had truly found the great love of my life. I was soon to find out just how much a man can love a woman.

FIRST DATE

First date stories can really be crazy. Some are both first and last dates. Some lead to a second, but then lead nowhere. My favorite first date story is from friends, Edith and Floyd, who were married for sixty years. The two first met on a blind date when her roommate convinced her to go on a date with her, her boyfriend, and his friend who was freshly discharged from the Navy. As she told the story, the evening began very well, because when they went to meet the boys her date turned out to be owner of a convertible, and she explained that that was a promising beginning. Off the two couples went to a movie. At that time in her life my friend was working an evening shift, and even though it was her night off from work, she was sleep deprived and fell asleep at the drive-in movie. After all those years of marriage they were still laughing about that first date. Clearly, sixty years later they were still love-struck. In fact, when in 2019 I officiated Floyd's funeral, I could not resist telling that wonderfully amusing story.

As was common after most of those Monday evening dinners with the singles group, several of us would gather at some restaurant or someone's house for a couple of hours of socializing, great laughs and telling stories. It was, as some say, a blast! Judy and I had gotten acquainted during those gatherings and I made a point of sitting with her at the dinners. In fact, it was at one those dinners that I knew we were at some point going to have a real date. I had placed my food plate on the table and returned to retrieve a dessert. Chocolate was smeared on the side of my hand as I returned to the table and when I reached for a napkin a voice from behind me asked, "would you like me to lick that off for you?" We all laughed, but I knew right then I was going to ask her out on a real date, in fact my good friend John (who was Chairman of the Deacons at the church I pastored) told me I would be a fool if I failed to ask her out. Truthfully, I never asked Judy out for a first date. She asked me, and some date it was to be. Judy was a member of the choir at her church and that choir was going to join with several other choirs in Nashville to form a massive choir for a service that was being held to officially appoint new missionaries to their assignments overseas. Sure...most are thinking...who wants to ride on a bus for a five hour round trip to go to a "church" meeting and listen to sermons and speeches and the commissioning of a large group of men and women to go traipsing off around the world? Now understand, it was a very important and impressive event. There were dignitaries present, high ranking officials in our Baptist denomination, and frankly, these missionaries were willing to risk their lives to take the gospel to those who had seldom or never heard the message. But make no mistake: I agreed to that evening for one reason—Judy. What? Did anyone really think I would miss the opportunity to sit next to her for four hours on that bus? Not surprisingly, Judy had arrived late, and the entire bus sat waiting on her. She was dressed to the nines, and I was captivated by the scent of her perfume. I later learned that it was new perfume just out in 1985 called "Beautiful," and she certainly was. We departed Chattanooga at 3:00 p.m. that afternoon and it was well past midnight when we returned. The round-trip bus ride was five hours long, and oh, how

I hate road trips. But I can attest that the ride sitting next to Judy was nothing less than rhapsody in my soul.

As I reflect on that evening, I am reminded of a Chuck Berry song that used to make Judy and me laugh. I always told her that song was written just for me. The song was *"No Particular Place to Go."* Those of another generation may need to check out the lyrics, but it was about a guy out cruisin' with a girl and their romantic walk was foiled by a faulty seat that would not cooperate. Despondent over a date ruined by a seat belt the guy bemoaned his fate and declared his lingering grudge against the device that prevented his romantic walk with that girl. As I drove home with Judy's scent still lingering in my imagination, in those wee hours of the morning I held a grudge against the bus driver for getting us home as soon as he did. However, it is a few of the lyrics from the Four Seasons' *Oh What A Night* that best captured my drive home. Like that song declares, I had been mesmerized by Judy and my head was spinning as I wished that the night had not ended.

Indeed, it had been...oh what a night! Other days and nights were in our future, but the memory of that first date lingers still. From her natural beauty to her enticing scent, those piercing eyes, along with her captivating laugh will forever

live in my soul. What I believed to be true that night proved to be right, God had brought this lovely creature onto my path, and we were meant to be. The lyrics from *Earth Angel* by Harry Waters, Jr. and Marvin Berry fully describe what had happened to me. I had fallen for this angel God had sent my way, and it would not be long before I knew I was in love with her. Yes, make no mistake, I was moonstruck!

2

THE TWILIGHT ZONE

"You unlock this door with the key of imagination. Beyond it is another dimension – a dimension of sound, a dimension of sight, a dimension of the mind. You're moving into a land of both shadow and substance, of things and ideas. You've just crossed over into the Twilight Zone." By the time I was fifteen the TV version of the show had run its course. Somehow, to this day, I can still hear the music….Da Da Dada Da Da DaDa…running through my head as Rod Serling tells all of us we are about to cross over into that other dimension called the Twilight Zone.

Nine months had passed since I first contacted our doctor regarding some observations I had about Judy's behavior. There was the episode where she could not remember how to count money. There had also been the day she got confused in the parking lot and could not immediately remember how to locate the entrance to the building. How about the clock? She could not read the dial on her watch. She might recognize the numbers that appeared on the face of the digital clock, but she had no idea what the numbers represented. Now we sat waiting for the neurologist to tome into the room, knowing there was a dark shadow following us around, knowing that Judy had a problem bigger than anything we had ever imagined, yet hoping to hear something hopeful, something encouraging from the doctor.

Did I see it coming? I have thought many times that I missed it. Yet did we? I had to press the doctors to even consider that something might be wrong. After all, Judy was only 54 years old and was a vibrant, beautiful woman. She excelled in business. She was a devoted Christian with a beautiful singing voice…and oh my, how she loved to sing! She was fully engaged in the life of our church. She doted over the grandchildren, demonstrated her gift of hospitality and mercy on a regular basis, and certainly kept me on the straight and narrow. After six months of agonizing testing and waiting, the verdict was in.

I have often said that on that day we entered the twilight zone, stuck somewhere between reality and denial. My Mister "fix-it" personality was slammed into the wall. What options, if any, awaited us. Would there be any return from this new, strange dimension?

HOW DID WE GET HERE?

The conversation began with a bit of casual banter, but quickly turned serious when the doctor's face changed. Suddenly his slight smile was upside down. Then the doctor turned and looked at Judy as these words, "I am sorry Mrs. Johnston," came across his lips. What followed was the confirmation of our worst fears. Alzheimer's Disease. Thus, began what would become a living nightmare that would play out over the next fifteen plus years. Dr. Matthew Kodsi spent much time and used great detail in explaining the outcome of the months of testing that Judy had endured. There had been the most basic test used in assessing memory loss, the MMSE (Mini Mental State Exam), lab tests of spinal fluid drawn from spinal taps, and a battery of many other tests, all culminating with a PET scan. That lengthy investigative process had consumed the months of

October through December, and now we were seated across from Dr. Kodsi on January 5, 2004. "I'm sorry Mrs. Johnston…we have no doubts that you have early onset Alzheimer's Disease" were his words. Numbing. Devastating. Yet not totally surprised.

There had been so many signs, although I managed, as did doctors, to brush them aside as stemming from other issues in Judy's life at the time.

Judy had been so excited when two years earlier we had opened two deli-type restaurants. We had formed a company through which those restaurants would operate, and Judy was the General Manager. Judy had worked along my side for almost ten years in building and developing the financial services business that I had begun in 1986. Her grit and determination, coupled with her effervescent personality, was a tremendous asset for the business. Her marketing skills were remarkable, and clients thoroughly enjoyed interacting with her, probably more so than they did with me. We worked side by side for more than eight years, and frankly, those were terrific years for both of us. That working relationship shifted when I agreed to additional leadership responsibilities within my role with our parent firm. They did not permit spouses to formally work together. However, she remained at my side and was unofficially an extension of my new role. I have never seen anyone who was better at "working" a room full of people, chatting, laughing, and leaving everyone feeling like they were the most important person in the entire room. While she relished doing that, she at the same time felt that there was more she could do with her talents. It was that sense that she had more to do, more to contribute, more to accomplish, that led us to open the restaurants. Some two years later, while having lunch together in one of our restaurants, that I would be forced to consider that some of the little things that had caught my casual attention, might need more specific attention.

Judy and I had agreed we would meet for lunch in the Hixson, TN location and it would be a good time for me to give her the payroll records and checks for both locations. Business was very, very good that day. We both always relished those type days. Customers kept coming and the lines were getting longer. Judy hopped up and like good leaders do, "rolled up her sleeves" and pitched in to speed up service. She relieved the employee at the cash register so that he could move over to the food prep line to facilitate the move of food orders more quickly to the register and to the customers. There it was!

ONE OF MANY

Sure, there had been little things, but don't we all miss a few things? Don't we forget some of the little details? Don't we all occasionally have distractions and concerns that detract from our focus? I had observed some changes, a few mishaps, that I chalked up to any number of things and events in our lives at the time. Judy's mother, who lived with us for almost seventeen years, had surgery following a brief illness. While in the hospital she had contracted a serious infection which (minus one week) led to a three month stay in the hospital. That alone would be enough to knock any of us off center. Judy had always been meticulous in managing our household finances, and there had been some minor hiccups. She had gotten lost inside the hospital, unable to locate her mother's room...but who hasn't had that experience? There was another significant event that I did not find out about until several years later. Judy called a friend to back her car out of the garage, explaining to the friend that she did not know how to back it out of the garage. Now, on this day in the restaurant, right in front of me...Judy was unable to count money as customers were paying her for their food orders. The electronic cash register made all the calculations and plainly displayed the amount of change due to the customer. Judy was unable to grasp what the numbers meant. For example, it might tell both the customer and her that $12.22 was due back to the customer, but she was completely unable to understand what to do next. In order to avoid further confusion and even embarrassment for Judy, I moved quickly to the register. But now I knew! We have something significant happening. Something that cannot be ignored.

CREATING URGENCY

In the late Spring of 2003, I wrote a lengthy letter to our family medical physician, Dr. Richard Peters. He had been our doctor for many years and knew us well, both medically and personally. In my letter I presented an outline of my observations of Judy's behavior and activities over the past several months. That letter spurred Dr. Peters to get Judy in for an appointment, and from that meeting arranged for Judy to have an MRI. Shortly after the MRI, I sat in our den and had just glanced at my watch and noted that it was 9:00 p.m. Church choir rehearsal would be ending soon, and Judy would be on her way home. My thoughts of her arrival were quickly interrupted by the music of the song, "Yea Alabama," the fight song of the University of Alabama, which served as the "ringtone" for my cell phone. Frankly, I don't remember getting many phone calls directly from a physician, yet, as I answered the phone on this particular Wednesday evening, I immediately recognized the voice as that of Dr. Peters. His report on Judy's MRI result was staggering. Dr. Peters expressed his total astonishment at what he was seeing in the scan…he began using words like atrophy, diminished, shrunken…unlike anything he had ever seen in a brain image of any person Judy's age. Just two months earlier we had had a party celebrating Judy's fifty-fourth birthday. I am sure I asked questions, probed for answers…but frankly, I cannot remember my verbal response. I do remember just sitting there, after the doctor hung up the phone, thinking this isn't real. This cannot be happening. What happens next?

A GOD THING

Late spring and early summer was spent with Dr. Peters in assessments and discussions about next steps. His recommendation to arrange an appointment for Judy with a local neurological group seemed to Judy and me to be a natural course of action. Judy and I would soon learn that yes, it was the natural thing to do, but it also had a very significant component as well.

Dr. Peters' nurse contacted us to inform us that an appointment had been made with the neuro with one of their senior partners. We were pleased to hear about the particular doctor and his experience and expertise, but there was a big problem. The pages of the calendar had now flipped to July, and the appointment was not to take place until November. Given our dispositions, and I am certain more me than Judy, we just could not fathom such a lengthy wait to see the neurologist. The angst of waiting and not knowing became intolerable. I am sure I badgered Dr. Peters' office to the point they finally agreed to try to persuade the group of neurologist to find some way to see Judy earlier. What happened next, we believed was truly a God thing.

At the time, just six years removed from graduating with a specialization in neurology from medical school, Dr. Matthew Kodsi was a new associate of the Chattanooga Neurological Associates. He was rather young, not (as they say here in the South) from "these parts," and in the early stages of developing a medical practice. Dr. Peters' nurse called to tell us that we could get in to see Dr. Kodsi if we did not wish to wait on one of their more seasoned doctors. Judy and I agreed that we wanted to make the appointment and see him as quickly as possible, and we found ourselves making our first visit to his office in September 2003. Dr. Kodsi proved himself to be a genuinely compassionate, caring, understanding human being. His medical knowledge and skills were equally evident. Judy bonded quickly with Dr. Kodsi and thus began a doctor patient relationship that would span almost sixteen years. In the early years, Judy was still very functional and would always want updates about his family, especially their love for cruises and Mickey Mouse...which often became one and same thing. Judy and I chose to believe that Dr. Kodsi came into our lives and our circumstances not by chance, but that our paths became intertwined for sixteen years because God brought a young doctor to Chattanooga, and God knew we needed that doctor to be a guide on a yet unknown journey into the Twilight Zone.

3

I'M NOT CRAZY

Judy's giggle quickly turned into full blown laughter, so much so that it jolted me from being lost in my own thoughts, and even as I sat with my hands gripping the steering wheel, I jerked my head around and glanced at Judy. Still laughing, and pointing to the radio in the car, she said, "Listen to that song! That's me!" The song was *I'm Not Crazy*. It talked about an individual who was not crazy, but impaired, and how before long everyone would see that person differently.

The release of that song, by Matchbox Twenty, almost coincided with Judy's diagnosis of dementia. There are numerous theories as to the meaning of the song, but clearly it was written to describe the mental angst of someone suffering from a mental breakdown or struggling with a mental disease. At the time Judy and I heard that song on the radio in our car, we had not had much to laugh about in many months. Mental health is not a laughing matter, but somehow it had struck Judy as funny, in a very serious way. At least that was my impression of her response. The words resonated with her, and the lyrics themselves made her laugh, yet she reasoned that those words had significant implications for the two of us.

THE STIGMA OF DEMENTIA

Dementia, of which Alzheimer's Disease is a type, will not likely be a topic of conversation at your next dinner party. For decades, the treatment of dementia often meant admission to an asylum. Dr. Alois Alzheimer, who is credited with the "discovery" of Alzheimer's, was a psychiatrist working in an asylum. I have observed that people, even those who themselves have the disease, or have a family member with dementia, seem almost embarrassed to talk about the disease. People seem to talk in hushed tones and whispers when revealing that either they, or some person they know has been diagnosed with dementia. I have entire conversations with people who have a family member struggling with Alzheimer's Disease, and dance around the name of the disease. It's almost as if refusing to call it what it is will make it not so, that it will just go away. I am convinced that dementia, and especially Alzheimer's Disease, has long been shoved into the corner by both clinicians and the community. Some of the response is due to a lack of knowledge and misunderstanding. However, there also continues to be a general perception that dementia is simply a problem for the elderly. Judy and I determined that we would never whisper about her diagnosis, rather we would speak loudly and clearly to anyone who would listen, and that we would work to gain the ear of anyone who might possess the ability to make a positive impact on Alzheimer's research, education, funding and support of families dealing with the disease.

A DARK DISEASE WITH NO SURVIVORS

Alzheimer's Disease is an irreversible, progressive disease of the brain that slowly destroys brain cells, and with it comes the slow loss of memory and thinking skills and eventually in its latter stages individuals lose the ability to respond to their environment, carry on a conversation and to control movement. Loss of speech can occur, and that is sometimes accompanied by the inability to swallow. Sadly, over the course of the last seven days of Judy's life, the inability to swallow became the critical event that lead to her death. German physician Dr. Alois Alzheimer was the first to research the unusual behavior of a female patient. She was age 51 and presented symptoms of senility. No plausible answers for her condition presented themselves during her lifetime. Following her death, Dr. Alzheimer performed an autopsy and it was then that he identified amyloid plaques and neurofibrillary tangles. These very anomalies remain the focus of researchers to this day in their quest of finding a way to stop or even slow down the progression of this dark, deadly disease. The world is waiting for the day when we can celebrate the first survivor of Alzheimer's.

THE STAGGERING STATISTICS

- Alzheimer's is the sixth leading cause of death in the U.S.
- More than 6 million people in the U.S. have Alzheimer's Disease.
- Current projections have that number reaching 16 million by 2050.
- In 2016 nearly 16 million family members and friends provided more than 18 million hours of unpaid caregiving assistance to those with Alzheimer's.
- Some 50 million people worldwide have dementia, and that number is expected to reach 131.5 million by 2050.
- In 2015, on a worldwide basis, the cost of treating dementia rose to $818 billion.
- Every 65 seconds someone in the U.S. develops Alzheimer's.
- Between 2000 and 2015 deaths from Alzheimer's increased by 123%.

Research continues but is often strapped by lack of funding. Our nation and our world may face a tsunami of casualties, cost and catastrophic outcomes in the coming years. It is only about ten years before the first millennials will be turning 49, the Gen Xers will be turning 65 and the first boomers will turn 84. Even darker days may lay ahead.

THE SOURCE OF ALZHEIMER'S

There are several forms of dementia, with Alzheimer's being the most common cause of dementia among older adults. Dementia varies depending on the type of changes taking place in the brain. Other forms of dementia include Lewy body dementia, frontotemporal disorders, and vascular dementia. Alzheimer's accounts for 60 to 80 percent of all cases of dementia, and vascular dementia, microscopic bleeding and blockage in the vessels of the brain, is the second most common cause of dementia. Medical research has found that it is not uncommon for a person to have mixed dementia, which is a combination of two or more dementias. In the very early stages of Dr. Kodsi's testing (September 2003) of Judy he speculated that her issue might be more related to a frontotemporal disorder rather than Alzheimer's. By the time he completed the PET scan of her brain (November 2003) all indications were that it was indeed Alzheimer's.

In simplistic terms, dementia is caused by damage to brain cells. The damage interferes with the ability of the brain cells to interact (talk) with each other. When those damaged cells can no longer communicate clearly with each other an individual's thinking, feelings and even behavior will be impaired. The human brain is the most remarkable and technologically advanced computer known to mankind. It is programmed to tell us when to breathe, to tell our heart to pump and even set the rhythm in our heart, and to process reams of information at high speed. The brain organizes, synthesizes, and memorizes. The brain counts, computes, coordinates, and communicates. It tells us when to rise and when to sit. It tells us when to sleep and when to awake. With our brain we see, we hear, we talk, and we walk. Little wonder the Psalmist said:

> "For it was you who created my inward parts;
> you knit me together In my mother's womb.

I will praise you, for I have been remarkably
and wondrously made." (Ps. 139: 13-14 CSB)

Medical science does not yet know what causes Alzheimer's. What is known is that plaques and tau tangles spread throughout the brain, and as that takes place, brain tissue shrinks significantly. My own very elementary explanation is that the tangles (think of jelly fish with little tentacles dangling down) float around in the brain and interfere with the transportation of nutrients to brain cells. When nutrients fail to reach the cells, the cells die. In more scientific terms plaques, which are abnormal clusters of protein, build up between nerve cells. Plaques form when protein pieces called beta-amyloid clump together. Beta-amyloid is "sticky" and over time builds into plaques. Clumps of plaque may block cell to cell communication at synapse. Dying and dead nerve cells contain tangles which are made up of twisted strands of another protein.

There is a prevalent theory that for individuals with "early-onset" Alzheimer's (those younger than age 65), a genetic mutation may be the cause. Judy was fifty-four years of age when she began those months of testing (July-November 2003) with Dr. Peters and Dr. Kodsi. The youngest person that I have personally met who was diagnosed with Alzheimer's was forty-four years of age. I have read reports and stories of a family in South America wherein a large percentage of the family has been diagnosed with Alzheimer's in their early to mid-thirties, and it is known to have been diagnosed as young as age thirty. Curiously, in Judy's family there was no family history that would seem to point to some genetic cause of the disease. Dr. Kodsi also explored the possibility of a head trauma that some researchers theorize can be a precursor of Alzheimer's. As a teenager, about age sixteen, Judy and a friend were in an automobile accident. It is important to note that at that time some cars had safety belts, and some did not. Judy was the passenger in the car and neither she nor the girl driving were wearing safety belts. Judy's injuries were not deemed serious enough to keep her hospitalized, but she had been thrown into the windshield with substantial force. Using today's knowledge, and based on the magnitude of the blow to Judy's head, it is likely that a more exhaustive examination would have led her to be placed in what has become known in college and professional sports as a "concussion protocol." We never knew, nor will we ever know, but given Judy's family history her head injury may very well have been what set in motion a disease that eventually took her life.

Alzheimer's Disease beginning beyond age 65 is known as "late-onset" Alzheimer's. This is the most common form of the disease. It may or may not run in families, and researchers are yet to find any particular gene that causes it. In other words, no one knows for sure why some people get it, and others don't. Currently scientists do appear to be making advances in understanding who and why a person may get the disease. By DNA testing, using the comparison of certain genes (PSEN1 or APOE) and their variants, researchers have developed testing which can determine a person's risk of developing late-onset Alzheimer's.

THE STAGES OF ALZHEIMER'S

Perhaps like me, you have heard others refer to dementia as senility or even senile dementia. Unfortunately, those terms are indicative of the widespread, but completely inaccurate belief that serious mental decline is a normal part of aging. The changes and decline that come with dementia bear no resemblance to "normal." There are clear and pronounced differences in the signs of normal aging and dementia. On average a person with Alzheimer's lives four to eight years after diagnosis, but can live as long as twenty years, depending on age at diagnosis and other factors such as other health conditions. Generally, Judy was in overall excellent health other than the diagnosis of dementia and lived almost sixteen years from the date of a formal diagnosis. The medicines that were being used to treat Alzheimer's in 2003 were Aricept (Donepezil), Exelon (Rivastigmine), and Razadyne (Galantamine). These three medicines have very similar properties. Around the world there were other drugs that had begun to be used and one of the more promising drugs was Namenda (Memantine), but during the months leading up to Judy's diagnosis Namenda was not available for purchase in the U.S. As the 2003 holiday season was fast approaching, the Food and Drug Administration had not yet approved Namenda for sale in the U.S. Dr. Kodsi believed that Namenda, which works differently in the brain than Aricept, Exelon, and Razadyne, held promise and would be a good addition to one of the already available drugs. We had information from reputable pharmaceutical dispensaries in Great Britain and Canada and we were in the process of arranging the purchase of Namenda. Judy's face lit up with excitement when Dr. Kodsi told us in November 2003 that the U.S. FDA approved Namenda, and although U.S. doctors were not permitted to write a prescription for the "new" drug until January 2004 we were relieved. On the first day that it was permissible Dr. Kodsi wrote the prescription and she and I made a dash for the pharmacy we customarily used. Judy's face sank with disappointment when the pharmacist said the drug, though approved, was not yet in inventory. I never knew how but will always be grateful that our pharmacist had the drug in his store in less than five days. Dr. Kodsi always told me that Judy's longevity past diagnosis stemmed from a combination of her otherwise good health genes, the meds, and the attention that was given to caring for her.

Some people with memory problems have what is called *Mild Cognitive Impairment* (MCI). With MCI a person has more memory problems than normal for their age (and other contributing factors related to health, education, etc.). The MCI may not interfere with a person's everyday life. Balance and movement difficulties often accompany MCI, and older people with MCI appear to be at a greater risk for Alzheimer's, though not all of them do. I have been diagnosed with MCI, apparently caused by a vascular event. Although I seem to have a bit more forgetfulness and make a few more mistakes, I don't spend time thinking about it and choose to live out God's purpose and calling for my life.

Early stage Alzheimer's (also called mild stage)—In the earliest stages, long before symptoms can be detected with available tests, plaques and tangles have already begun to form in certain areas of the brain. At this early stage, those areas involved include learning and memory, along with thinking and planning. It is at this stage that a person continues to function independently. Driving, working, daily functioning, and socializing typically appear normal. Yet, the person may feel as if he or she is having memory lapses. Once familiar words may suddenly become difficult. The location of everyday objects may become an oft repeated struggle. It is common for this person to have increasing trouble with planning and organizing. Names may suddenly be an ongoing challenge. Those who are in closest contact will likely be the first to notice the changes, while individuals who have less frequent contact may not yet be in tune with what is happening. Remember, some changes could have begun twenty or more years prior to diagnosis.

Middle stage Alzheimer's (also called moderate stage)—Professionals state that this is typically the longest stage and can last for many years. Naturally, the person with Alzheimer's will require an increasing level of care. The person in middle stage Alzheimer's may remember significant details about their life but will have greater difficulty performing tasks. Damage to nerve cells in the brain now make it difficult to express thoughts and complete routine tasks. He or she may express anger or frustration and to even demonstrate behaviors that are totally uncharacteristic. Common symptoms in this stage include forgetting once common information (address, birthday, phone number), the ability to select appropriate clothing, mood changes, trouble controlling bladder and bowels, change in sleep patterns, and the risk of wandering and becoming lost. In general, this stage lasts from two to ten years.

Late state Alzheimer's (also called severe stage)—It is in this final stage that the person loses the ability to respond to their surroundings and will have little to no awareness of recent experiences. This stage brings with it the necessity of round-the-clock assistance with all activities, including those of personal care and hygiene. Though they may remain capable of saying words or phrases, they are incapable of carrying on a conversation. A decline in physical health becomes a prominent issue and infections become common, and the risk of pneumonia is high. This phase is generally thought to last one to five years.

My personal experience was that there were not clear lines drawn between the stages. Judy remained very functional for at least two plus years. I later learned that she had experienced some mishaps and friends came to her rescue during that early period. We managed to continue for several years many of our favorite hobbies, traveling and tailgating at football games. None of what we did was particularly easy, and nothing was done without regard for all accommodations that Judy would need. We continued to dine out on a regular basis, even though I had to feed Judy her food. Not once was I embarrassed by the glances of others, and Judy was totally unaware of their stares. On a return trip from Florida to Chattanooga we stopped in Valdosta, Georgia for a meal. While in the restaurant Judy needed to use the restroom, and there was no so-called family restroom available. I rewarded our server handsomely to assist Judy, and at the same time swore to myself I would never put Judy in that situation again. I bought a customized van that included a kitchen, sofa bed, and a full bathroom. You see, although I had a professional career, job one was Judy and having her experience all that we squeeze out of our life together.

THE SYMPTOMS OF ALZHEIMER'S

Lists are in abundance as to what one might look for in considering inexplicable changes in behavior, thinking and reasoning skills. As we consider some of the so-called signs and symptoms of Alzheimer's Disease, it is important to remember that with some of the "signs" there will be some similarities with typical age related changes, but at the same time it is not difficult to see the differences. For example, one early sign of Alzheimer's is memory loss that has begun to disrupt the life of the individual. This could include forgetting important dates and events, not recalling recently learned information, or asking the same question over and over. Now some of you are thinking, "oh gosh, I do that." However, it is likely simply age-related change if when those moments occur you later remember the person's name or the event or the appointment.

Other signs could include:

- Struggling with problem solving and planning activities – may include using a recipe, paying bills, working with numbers. This was the first thing about Judy that caught my attention. I'm certain there were earlier signs, but this issue was so remarkably different that it could not be ignored.
- Familiar tasks become difficult – this would certainly include driving to familiar locations and performing routine tasks.
- Confusion with time and place – dates, time, and the passage of time. It can even include confusion with where they are or how they got there.
- Trouble with visual images and spatial relationships – In Judy's case this became so obvious in her closet. She loved clothes and had lots of clothes, and she was always beautiful in them. Shapes can be so troublesome for a person with Alzheimer's, and for Judy the triangle shape was something she just couldn't quite figure out. So, I would go in her closet from time to time and "fix" the clothes she had placed on hangers (yes, typically triangles). Judy, once so meticulous about hanging her clothes, had no idea that what she attempted to do did not begin to resemble what she had always done. Frankly, I knew not to try to show her or tell what to do. So, I would just watch her do it, and once she was out of the room I would return to the closet and re-hang her clothes.
- Problems with speaking or writing – Writing for Judy became impossible shortly following her diagnosis. Her signature was just a swirling, squiggly movement of her hand, which by the way, even when I placed her hand on the line requiring the signature, never stayed near the line as her hand ran up or down the page. Speech became more

halting and difficult over the passing of time. Remarkably, long after speech consisting only of single words now and then, she could still sing entire songs.

- Poor judgment and decreased decision-making ability.
- Isolation – become more withdrawn, difficulty at work or social settings.
- Personality and mood changes - includes confusion, depression, fearfulness, heightened anxiety, becoming suspicious of once familiar people or places

Things like genetics cannot be changed, and the process of aging is, well, something that I personally hope to continue to do for a long time to come. But in a research report presented at the 2019 Alzheimer's Association International Conference it was strongly suggested that the following may decrease the risk of cognitive decline and Alzheimer's: adopting a healthy lifestyle, to include healthy diet, not smoking, participating in regular exercise, and maintaining some form of cognitive stimulation.

By the way, Judy was not crazy. She had, however, become unwell.

4

WHEN A MAN LOVES A WOMAN

About two months before Judy graduated from high school, Percy Sledge, an Alabama-born balladeer with a wonderful, soulful sound, released a song that captures my heart when it comes to thoughts of Judy…it became one of the best loved songs in the history of soul. That song was, of course, *When A Man Loves A Woman*. Like Percy in the song, I was willing to do anything, and spend everything, to hold on to the woman I loved. My heart and mind had been eternally captured by what surely was the most beautiful creature God had ever made.

In the Spring 2016, in a telephone conversation with Judy's brother Roy, we were talking about the endless progression of Alzheimer's to destroy Judy's life. There had been a recent period of several days in which Judy had great difficulty in swallowing. In fact, we began to puree all her food in an attempt to get nourishment into her system, into her body. But that food, and even the liquids, had become a significant issue, to the extent that the physician sought me out and discussed the use of a feeding tube. My greatest fear was forming right before my eyes. Judy and I had both agreed, and we recorded it in a Living Will (Advanced Directive), as to the type of end-of-life treatment we wished to have for each of our benefit. Clearly, if it was an end of life decision, a feeding tube was not something either of us desired. The doctor's expression never changed when I informed him of what was contained in Judy's Living Will, and his only response was, "good decision." Remarkably, that episode lasted less than three days and Judy began to eat and drink once again. Perhaps selfishly, I had been praying that Judy and I would get to celebrate our thirtieth wedding anniversary. May 2 was now only a few weeks away and I was communicating to Roy all that had just happened to Judy, and perhaps now, even though she would not really know it, we would have that celebration after all. Like Percy's song, I was willing to spend all I had, just trying to hold on. We did celebrate that anniversary, and twelve months later another one. However, just four months after that 31st anniversary the inability to swallow would return, and this time even though I kept trying to hold on to her love, that dark, dreadful disease took her from me.

TOO GOOD TO BE TRUE

That bus trip date to Nashville was followed by much more time being spent with Judy. The cold of winter became the chill of spring, and before the eventual soaring heat of summer, Judy and I were spending time together almost every day. A couple of stanza's of Frankie Valli's hit, *Can't Take My Eyes Off You* expresses how captivated I had become with Judy, and being with her, hearing her voice, looking into her eyes…and yes, kissing those lips. Could it be

true? Could heaven be bringing us together? All I know is that I could not possibly get too much time in her presence. I knew that heaven meant us to be, and I was obviously smitten by just being in Judy's presence. Had we been teenagers, others would have surely said of us, "Judy and Alan are going steady."

MEET THE PARENTS

You remember Greg Focker in the movie *Meet the Parents*, right? Greg was madly in love with Pam and is getting ready to ask Pam to marry him when he decides to wait and ask her in front of her family. Then bam! The airline loses the luggage carrying the engagement ring. Things only get worse from that moment forward. Pam's Dad, not hiding his distaste and suspicions of Greg, uses covert operations strategies to investigate Greg and the entire trip becomes Greg's worst nightmare. It is knee slapping, hilarious comedy, but only when it's not "you" playing the role of Greg. Now I am not implying that I was being treated like Greg by Judy's family, but I am adamantly saying I was more than a little concerned about meeting Mary.

Judy was the youngest of five children. I had already met her two brothers David and Roy, and they were fun to spend time with. Judy and I had already spent enough time around the two of them that I felt very comfortable being with them. There was the sister, Helen. She and her husband had, because of his career, spent many years overseas and I knew I would meet her eventually, but that would be no time soon. Judy's father had died eight years earlier and her mother was currently living with and providing care to a very sick life-long friend, so I knew that was a box I would eventually have to check off, but that time would not be soon. That left just Mary.

Mary was the oldest of the five children. She was eighteen years older than Judy, and Mary and my mother shared the same birth month, and day of the month...in the same year! Mary and my mother were born on the same day, in the same year. Are you getting the picture yet? The test I was going to have to pass was not Judy's mother, it was getting past Mary. Compounding my worries was all those times Judy had told me about how Mary was always asking questions about me, to the extent that Judy once even used the word, "interrogation." Interrogation! I had even heard Judy's side of some of those telephone conversations with Mary. Oh goodness, what could Mary have been asked that would prompt Judy to say, "I am being careful?"

D-day arrived, Labor Day 1985… surely a family cook-out would be a safe environment for Judy and me to get together with her family, even if it was to be at Mary and Steve's (Mary's husband) house. The back yard was full of people, all of them kin to Judy, mostly trying to be nice to me. After what seemed like days of curious glances and so, so many questions, most of the crowd began to leave for their own homes. But not us. Judy and I were planning to remain for a little while but, the little while turned into several three hours. The evening was going so well. Mary and Steve were gracious hosts and it seemed to me that I was being able to satisfy, or at least tamp down, some of their concerns about Judy's relationship with me. Then it happened. The University of Alabama Crimson Tide was about to play the University of Georgia Bulldogs on television. Before we arrived at the cook-out I had made sure Judy knew that I wanted us to leave before the kick-off, primarily so that she and I could watch the game without an audience. Sure, being alone with Judy was always wonderful, but that was not the primary reason. You see, I change when Alabama lines up and tees up the football. No, not a change like Clark Kent running into a phone booth and charging out as Superman. More like when Dr. Jekyll morphs into Mr. Hyde, or the night turns to darkness and some vampire comes out to find his next victim. When the Alabama football team is playing, I'm out for blood. Any team playing Alabama is the enemy and must be soundly squashed. Now here I am, stuck at Mary and Steve's house and I am not about to miss watching the football game. It was quickly obvious that I cared more about the game than anyone else in the room. Most of them were Tennessee fans, plus a couple of Bulldog fans. Tense would be an understatement for the ebb and flow of the game. Alabama seemed to have the game under control when disaster struck. The final minute of the game was exhausting and exhilarating, all wrapped up in sixty seconds of time. Leading 13-9, Bama lined up to punt the ball...and disaster struck. The punt was blocked and rolled end over end until it rolled into the end zone. Georgia recovered it in the end zone for a touchdown. By then the vampire had come out, and while I can neither confirm nor deny, I was reminded for years to come, that I might have said a few un-preacher-like words. Now with only 50 seconds remaining to play, Alabama suddenly trailed 16-13. The Bama quarterback was a "kid" named Shula who had only about sixty passing yards for the entire game, and now following the kickoff, with only 50 seconds remaining to play, Alabama sat 65 yards from the end zone. What followed is the stuff of fairytales. The first play was an agonizing incompletion, but then came passes that seemed to go zip-zip-zip-touchdown! My reaction became enshrined in the lore and legends of Judy's family. With no thought of anyone around me, nor of where I was, I simultaneously jumped up from my chair, with what was reported to be an earsplitting, demonstrative, if not bloodcurdling scream, and in the same moment and movement jumped straight up. Not just up, but high enough so that my arms, extended straight up signaling a touchdown, got caught in the ceiling fan. Caught up in the exhilaration of the moment I was celebrating in what was a somewhat "normal" fashion for me. I was oblivious to both sounds and sights that had suddenly exploded in the room and now as I looked around the room all I saw was wide-eyed people who appeared to be momentarily caught between wonder and fear. Judy and I were married for more than three decades and I must have heard that story a thousand times. Steve regaled in telling that story every time he had an audience. I heard that story so much that I repeated the story myself when I officiated Steve's funeral some thirty years after the incident first happened.

Judy's mom's actual name was Elzora, but I called her Mrs. Ab (short for Abercrombie). She was such a sweet and endearing person, and she and I hit it off from the beginning. Judy's father had been a church music director, and Judy and all her siblings had great talent and loved to sing. Mrs. Ab and I had so much in common when it came to church music...we both loved it but could not sing,

I mean, not one note. Mrs. Ab lived with us for some seventeen years and she loved my Judy as much as I did, and I know for a certainty that she loved me as though I were her own son. She had grown up in Moundville, Alabama, a small town about fifteen miles from Tuscaloosa. There would be no need for me to fret over trying to convert her into a University of Alabama fan, for she already was a fan. She lived to be over 99 years old, and I can assure you that not once did she falter in her love for Judy, the Atlanta Braves, or the University of Alabama.

Judy's introduction to my family was void of any drama. My parents, who were still living in Alabama at the time, had come to Chattanooga for a weekend visit. Judy and I had had a few dates, but it had not yet officially developed into a steady  relationship, at least not for Judy. We all met up on the University of Tennessee-Chattanooga campus for an outdoor party. There was a lot of food, music, dancing, and a lot of people. As soon as Judy saw my parents and me arrive, she came bouncing over, gorgeous as always, and as the setting sun was reflecting in her beautiful, dancing eyes, she proved her charm to Mom and Dad. Judy came and went throughout the evening, mixing with all her friends; after all, she had a date for the party, but it wasn't me. Later in the evening as I was helping a group of guys pack up and load party leftovers into various vehicles Judy had returned to talk with my parents. Pointing to a man who was also loading cars, Judy said, "see that guy over there, that's my date tonight." She then turned and pointed to another and said, "but that's the guy I really want to be with." I, along with my parents, was in the car headed home from the party when Mother told me that story. By the way, that other guy was me, and both of my parents made it clear to me that I should not do anything to mess this up. Clearly, they too already loved Judy.

TILL DEATH DO US PART

Judy and that "other guy" had many dates over a period of about twenty-six months. We grew even more deeply in love, and our dates were fun, adventurous, filled with intrigue, and sometimes a little crazy. There had been a whitewater rafting trip that saw one of our raft mates jump from the raft into the river. There were all those UTC basketball games. Dinners, movies, theatre, concerts, mountain hikes, beach trips, and football games filled our weekends and date nights. Those months were not without some drama along with lots of bumps and bruises. Judy had surgery and that was followed by the loss of her job. I had completely changed careers. Although I loved the great church I was then pastoring, I resigned and began a career in business as a financial planner. My two daughters, then ages fourteen and ten, were less than enthusiastic about my relationship with Judy. Heck, to tell the truth, they were at times outright rude and hostile to Judy. Buckets of tears were shed by Judy over those girls. Judy, who was never able to have children of her own, did in fact love my daughters, Joy and Jennifer, as much as she could have ever loved any child that she might have given birth to herself. Thankfully, the passing of time changed their relationship with Judy and long before my children were adults, they fully knew and acknowledged that Judy was far more than a stepmother, more than just Dad's wife, she was family. Later in our lives Judy and I found such great joy in our grandchildren, and oh my how Judy loved them, and they returned that love to her. She was, and will forever be, grandmother to Katie, Maggie, and Alex.

On May 2, 1987 I was standing in that same church parking lot where I had stood twenty-six months earlier waiting for Judy to arrive so we could board that bus for the trip to Nashville. Reaching for the door that would lead me into the chapel of that church I was thinking about the adventure that had filled my life now for these past two years. That adventure had a name…Judy. Just this past Christmas I had surprised Judy by asking her to marry me…and she said yes! Only minutes remained before I would say "I do," and

33

with those two little words become the luckiest, most blessed man on the face of the earth.

Earlier, in January 1986, I had begun a financial services business. By the time I retired in 2019 I had an almost thirty-four year career, and it was the very embodiment of a statement found in the Bible in Ephesians 3:20 which says in part, "...who is able to do far more abundantly than all we can ask or think..." It was a bold leap of faith for me to resign from my pastorate and to dive headlong into a new career, especially a career in financial services. I believed then, and I know now with the greatest certainty, that it was God who directed me and who opened all the right doors for me to enter that field. Furthermore, just as much as I know that I also know that God brought Judy into my life, and Judy became my partner in the business. She worked in the office with me for many years, and beyond that she was my motivation and inspiration. She was a tremendous asset to our business and played a large part in attracting clients and new business. In the sixteen-month period leading up to our wedding day, Judy and I had an agreement about work and dates. My work weeks averaged about sixty or more hours each week and even weeknights were spent either in appointments or preparing for the next day's appointments. Wednesday nights were kept open to attend midweek church services, and often I returned to work after those services. Friday was date night with a caveat...if I had someone who wanted to see me...and, if that person was likely to write a check...our date began when that appointment ended. Now that's what you call an understanding girlfriend. We still laughed about that long after we were married. Oh goodness, all the memories of all those wonderful times still bring such joy, and yes, those same memories serve as medicine, a consolation of sorts, when I begin to feel the deep sadness of her absence.

Wedding anniversaries should be celebrations, and ours were always exciting, and at times even exotic. For us, they became experiences. Our sixteenth anniversary had recently passed with a bit less fanfare due to Judy's mother's illness and extended stay in the hospital. We had celebrated, but it did not measure up to our usual extravaganza. Judy had been dividing her time between the restaurants we owned, the hospital, and home. Just three months earlier I had purposefully removed myself from my role as a field Vice President for American Express Financial Advisors. That decision meant no more days and nights traveling for business, and with that decision, my singular purpose became focusing on individual client needs. At the time, when that decision was made, I only knew that I was tired of weary nights in hotels, and too much time away from Judy. Now, looking back, I know that it was God's way of preparing me for what was to come. What was to come began with that Wednesday night phone call from Dr. Richard Peters, and the report he had for me regarding Judy's MRI results.

I had rather "take a beating" than to spend a day at an amusement park. Sure, I've been many times. I took my daughters when they were young, and then after the grandkids came along Judy and I were once again off to the parks. When my children were young, we would visit a nearby amusement park named Lake Winnepesaukah. Mind you, I did not at all mind riding the "Tea Cup" with them. It would spin around and around at a moderate rate of speed. We would then eventually work our way to the back of the park, and it was there that one of my greatest fears resided…a rollercoaster. The one at Lake Winnie was aptly named the Cannonball. It rose well above the clouds (not really, it just seemed that way to me) and moved at more than 100 miles per hour (another not really, well… you get the idea). It zipped around really, really fast and made hairpin turns that would turn your knuckles white, and then your stomach would be left at the top as coasters rocket like ascent to the top suddenly became a free fall toward what would end in my certain demise. Of course, it always ended without incident, but I can still hear the clackety-clack sound of the Cannonball as it barreled its way up and around that wooden framed track. It was not fun then, and I still hate it. On that Wednesday night in June 2003 I boarded a coaster ride far more frightening that the Cannonball, one that would not allow me off for more than fifteen years.

The memories of those fifteen years bring to me an odd concoction of smiles and tears, joy and sadness. Judy loved me so deeply, and I loved her both intensely and immensely. Nothing ever changed that, and a long battle with Alzheimer's Disease never diminished my love for her. Alzheimer's did change, in many ways, how I was able to express my love for Judy. I never imagined on the day that I said "I do" that I would need to learn how to do everything for another adult. As the disease robbed Judy more and more of her abilities, I became more and more determined that for as long as possible I would make her life as enjoyable, comfortable, and as stable as humanly possible. Over the course of time Judy lost her ability to walk, talk, feed herself, use her hands, bath and groom herself, or any of the other hundreds of things that we each do every day without so much as a thought. I learned how to apply Judy's makeup, because I knew that would have been important to her. I even became pretty good at that job, including eyeliner and lipstick. Even though I kept trying, I never really mastered the eye mascara. My heart is as pure as the driven snow when I state that it was my honor to do that for Judy. Percy sang it, "if she is bad, he can't see it, she can do no wrong." The Apostle Paul said it, "love bears all things, endures all things, love never ends." Gosh, I love that woman so much.

Judy was both beautiful and remarkable. I counted myself the luckiest guy in the world to have Judy at my side and in my heart. Just being in her presence was nothing short of glorious. What can I say? Her personality, her charm, her scent, her beauty, her grace, and grit all linger in my mind.

Her spirit is close by, I can sense her. I miss her! I can close my eyes, and what I see is Judy, pure poetry in motion, like Johnny Tillotson described in his song *Poetry in Motion*. Judy was gifted with natural beauty, and there was also an unmistakable grace and charm about her. My eyes could not but help follow her every time she swayed across a room. Even yet, I close my eyes and see her gliding across the room.

5

BAD THINGS HAPPEN TO GOOD PEOPLE

Though in the ministry for more than fifty years, I am still baffled by God. The book of Psalms in the Bible is full of questions—questions I am asking God even centuries after those Psalms were written. Questions full of why, how, when, who that often seem to come with far too few answers. Too often I am left wondering if God took a day off. Then there are those times in my total misunderstanding of God that I am filled with grief, and dare I say it, even angry. Bad things happen to good people and it is disturbing. Why do innocent children get sick and die? Why do some families never seem to catch a break, while others seem to live a charmed life? Why do we continue to murder the unborn? Why did six million Jews die at the hand of an evil, deranged mad man? On Easter Sunday 2019 there were 300 Christians who were attacked and killed in Sri Lanka, why? Why did my Judy have to be diagnosed with Alzheimer's? Why, why, why? I am still waiting on a lot of answers. I still have even more questions. Theologically I understand the concept of good and evil. I get that. But then there is all the suffering that comes with it, and at times I stand drop-jawed before God wondering why. I suppose there is a measure of solace to be found when, in the Bible, we can read about so many who came long before us, who had the same intellectual and spiritual struggles that we often experience. It was the woman Naomi, in the book of Ruth, who had to bury her husband and her two sons. In deep anguish and emotional honesty, she asked God if he considered her His enemy? In her anguish she said "...*my life is much too bitter for you to share, for the Lord's hand has turned against me.*" (Ruth 1:13 CSB) Sometime life brings great sorrow and bitterness, and we often don't find ready answers to all of our "why's.

THROUGH IT ALL

In the early years following Judy's diagnosis she and I had many long conversations, and many long prayers as we both struggled to understand what God was doing in our lives. Frankly, Judy's faith was stronger than mine. Yes, she had fears. Fear of the unknown. Fear of the known. Fear of forgetting those she loved most. I know that she and my mother spent hours talking and praying and reasoning with God. Friends have told me that they too had conversations with Judy about the impending darkness of Alzheimer's that could, and likely would, rob us of the person we all knew and loved. Yet, it was Judy who was so remarkably strong, confident, and assured of her faith that God was sovereign, and that He would see all of us through the dark valley that lay ahead. In fact, one evening as we sat in the den at our house she began to sing, and it was Andrae' Crouch's song, *Through It All*. The song talks about tears, sorrow and so many questions for God. For Judy, just as the song says, all of the changes and circumstances brought on by the disease had made her faith stronger. Her faith never faltered; it only grew more fervent. There are several verses of that song, as well as the chorus lines repeating themselves, but it ends with the final verse which somehow encapsulates Judy's faith in God and helped keep her joy intact. It points to the storms that life can bring, with all of the ups and downs of the emotional roller coaster. But Judy's testimony was that of the song, that there was nothing that caught God by surprise, and that He would see her through it all.

By the time Judy finished singing that song in its entirety she too was crying, and I was an emotional wreck. More tears were going to come our way, but Judy was rock solid in her faith in God.

A NAGGING QUESTION

Loss and suffering are ever present. The pain that comes with loss and suffering is a common thread in the human experience. At this very moment, all across the globe, the world seems to be shut down by a pandemic known as COVID 19. Businesses are closing. Jobs are being lost. Income is being taken away. Citizens are being told to "shelter-in-place," meaning to stay in your homes and don't venture out. Some are dying and life for all of us has been turned upside down. Wars, floods, hurricanes, divorces, death of loved ones, loss of health...the losses mount up, the suffering continues, and answers for our questions remain elusive. The oldest book in the Bible is the book of Job, and when one begins to ask serious questions about human suffering it is difficult to not first think of Job. Job was a man who, according to the Bible, sought to do everything that he could do to please God. Yet his world collapsed before his eyes. Wife, children, livelihood, savings, business, health...all gone! Why? Job's experience, if nothing else, makes it clear that our very existence has a significant spiritual component to it, and with that truth comes many unanswered questions. Such experiences can leave us empty, fragile, and feeling isolated. I can relate to it all. It's like being in a boat that is taking on water and you are working frantically to bail water from the boat , then realizing that your efforts will never be enough to prevent the boat from capsizing. A group of men traveling with Jesus had that very experience.

CHASING STORMS

Storm Chasing Adventure Tours...that's what the advertisement says. It goes on to say *Chase with the pros...Storm chasing in Tornado Alley.* The website goes on to explain what a typical day might look like once you sign up for your adventure with the pros. What kind of adrenaline junkie goes looking for that kind of trouble? Geez, I've seen up close and personal what a tornado can do. Back in the early 1970's while pastoring and living in Coffeeville, Alabama, we hunkered down in our house while just such a storm had our house in its direct path. The parsonage and one other house, along with the church building, all sat alone on a little roadway near town. My study was located in the parsonage and I was in the study when I noticed that the big oak trees were no longer waving in the wind but were now twisting in the wind. Walking out onto the front porch, which faced west, I was stricken with terror. Coming in the distance was a terrifying, boiling, black funnel, and it was bearing down on our house. Screaming, I rushed my family to the back corner of the house, which also happened to be the lowest position in the house. Our family became a huddled prayer meeting of three.

Such storms are often deadly. In the Tuscaloosa, Alabama tornado of 2011, a storm that stretched 1.5 miles wide and had a duration of more than 1.5 hours, 64 lives were taken, and much of that city and surrounding communities were obliterated. The twisting winds, reaching almost 200 miles per hour, left a path of devastation and death. Such storms can also be random and inexplicable. I saw a photograph of a house that was demolished by the winds, leaving only two things behind. The concrete slab remained, as did the china cabinet which had been in the dining room. The cabinet sat there in pristine condition, with no glass broken, as if nothing had happened.

On Easter Sunday 2020 I found myself once again huddled in a house, this time in a bathroom, as an EF-3 tornado ripped into our neighborhood in Chattanooga, Tennessee. In the aftermath of the storm, lives were lost, including that of a four-year-old child. Homes and businesses were destroyed. Schools and churches were obliterated. Again, the question comes, "why do such things happen?"

Our family prayer meeting of three survived that storm in Coffeeville that had us in the crosshairs. The house which had been located across the street was lifted off its foundation moved over the edge of the street, and the forest behind our house was ripped into toothpicks. The parsonage had a few shingles missing and the television antenna was bent. So, I am going to leave the storm chasing to those like Helen Hunt in the 1996 movie *Twister*, and those who sign up for the storm chasing adventure tour.

TILL THE STORM PASSES BY

The Bible does nothing to camouflage or distort reality. Life does not always seem fair. People get sick, they hurt, they die. The Bible says it rains on the good and the bad. In an attempt to make some sense out of life, especially my journey with Judy, I made a list of storms in the Bible. I'm sure there are more, but I came up with at least three dozen references to storms. Two of those references captured my attention.

The first is found in Acts 27 and it presents quite the adventure. The Apostle Paul and a traveling companion are in route to Rome and as part of their travels they booked passage on a ship. In reading the story in its entirety my mind may have wandered off to the television show *Gilligan's Island*. In the television show a small group of people shoved off for a three hour tour, but then they were shipwrecked. It was fifteen years of episodes before Gilligan and his friends were rescued. For the Apostle Paul what began as an ordinary trip, one that found favorable south winds, soon encountered a raging typhoon capable of capsizing the ship, resulting in lost cargo and the potential for many lost lives among the crew and passengers. This story contains many lessons, not the least of which is that no matter how the winds are blowing, God remains in control of everything. Theologians refer to that as the Sovereignty of God. All authority resides in God and emanates from God. When storms arise, we, like the sailors on that ship, tend to look for answers in all the wrong places. In fact, this Acts 27 story gives us a textbook case in what not to do when fearful and stormy times arrive in our lives. The hasty, ill advised, actions of the sailors could have been calamitous had it not been for the intervention of

Paul. The advice of the expert (the captain of the ship) almost cost them their lives, but not one life was lost when they finally turned to the godly advice of Paul.

The second of those two captivating scriptures is found in Mark 4: 35-41; 5:1. Here we join Jesus, now exhausted after a busy day of teaching and ministry, and he asked his closest followers, the disciples, to join him in a boat so that they could cross the lake (Sea of Galilee) for a bit of rest. What follows is quite remarkable. As is seen in the scripture a storm arose and the occupants, minus one, soon feared for their lives.

Judy and I were already Christians when we met. She came from a very musically inclined family and her own musical talents were remarkable. I was licensed as a Baptist minister when I was eighteen years old and I cannot remember a time when church was not an integral part of my life. Once she and I married we naturally joined the same church, Central Baptist Church in Hixson, Tennessee. Our faith as Christians and our involvement in church came as naturally to us as breathing. Prayers, reading the Bible, attending church, fellowshipping with our Pastor Ron Phillips and his wife Paulette, as well as with many other friends, were more important than ever as Alzheimer's continued its invasion of Judy's brain. Our Bible class at church became more and more supportive as the weeks became months and the months became years. Judy and I could not have found a more loving group of people to share our lives with. I do not think we could have survived the storm which was bearing down on us had it not been for our faith, and for the family of faith who climbed into the boat with us just as the winds of the storm began to rock our world. Based on Mark 4, here are a few thoughts and observations.

POWERFUL STORMS

As we read in Mark 4:37, it is clear that a powerful, (*"And a great windstorm arose..."*) unexpected, storm blew in on the little crew in the boat.

It is rather common for *sudden storms* to appear on the Sea of Galilee. Sudden squalls occur as winds swirl from the mountain and dive to the sea below, because it sits about six hundred feet below sea level. I personally have been on the Sea of Galilee several times and can provide first-hand testimony of how quickly such storms arise. With only slight waves lapping at the shoreline and the glistening sun dancing off the surface of the water, Judy and I donned our sunglasses and boarded the boat. With a bright sun and an almost cloudless sky, we launched from a small harbor in Galilee on route to Capernaum. In search of lunch, birds stayed busy diving into the wake being left behind our boat as we plowed through the water. Judy was thrilled to be out on the Sea of Galilee. One of my favorite photographs captures the two of us dancing on the deck of the boat as it made it way toward Capernaum. On one of my Sea of Galilee adventures we were two thirds of the way across the lake when a sudden storm appeared with winds and waves that buffeted the boat enough to cause the crew to move everyone off the decks and into the boat where they quickly closed the windows. The storm, which appeared seemingly out of nowhere, was gone almost as quickly as it came. Frequent travelers in that region know that the possibility of sudden storms always exist, and in the same way most of us have learned that life is just as apt to be hit with sudden, powerful storms. We encounter storms of sickness, storms of misfortune, storms of disappointment, storms of rejection, financial storms, emotional storms…the list seems at times to be endless. Although the seeds of Alzheimer's had likely begun long ago in Judy's brain, perhaps even as a teenager, we were living our dream when Dr. Kodsi gave us the diagnosis and explained what we could expect. Suddenly nothing else mattered. Suddenly we could think of little else. Suddenly no amount of resources or education prepared us for this storm.

For the disciples in that boat with Jesus that storm which came so suddenly was also a very *severe storm*. The Bible refers to it as a "great" storm. The Message Bible states it this way, "*A huge storm came up. Waves poured into the boat, threatening to sink it.*" Remember, many of the disciples were fishermen, men of the sea. They had been out on that water many times and endured many storms. But now the boat was in danger of sinking! Many can relate to the disciples in that very moment. For them it was the wind, the waves, the sea. For Judy and me it was the diagnosis and the doctors' visit. Many others have shared that experience with us. For others, the moment came with the ringing of the doorbell or a phone call that jolts you out of your sleep. That sudden jolt of hearing a bad report, a bad diagnosis, or a missed or lost opportunity. Sudden and severe storms can rage in on us with our dear families, our careers, our friends, our hopes, and dreams. Few are immune.

Without a question the disciples of Jesus were also suddenly in a *serious storm*. When I read their reaction and response to their perceived inactions of Jesus, I can envision them scurrying around as they tried to bail water out of the boat. Perhaps they tied a rope around themselves in hopes of avoiding being washed overboard. Though I have been on ocean voyages, I have never had that kind of experience. Judy and I were once aboard an airplane that had a very serious issue, and the crew was hastily preparing all we passengers for an emergency landing. We were told that the airplane did not have any operating landing gear and that the runway would be foamed in advance of our landing. Amidst the chaotic atmosphere, especially when we all tucked our heads between our knees for the landing, I readily admit that I thought, we may die. I am certain of one thing in this story from the Bible, those disciples were all thinking and perhaps even shouting, "we may die." Life eventually brings all of us to those troubled waters, brimming with the unknown, the uncertain. What we do next always determines the outcome.

PERPLEXING QUESTIONS

Mark's account next brings us, in verse 38, to a most perplexing question. The disciples, reaching the point of desperation shook Jesus awake and asked, *"do you not care that we are perishing?"*

I have no problem at all in imagining the *fear of the disciples.* Their circumstances were dire. The storm was growing stronger. The boat continued to take on water as it was rocking and rolling with every blast of wind. Let's face it, they feared for their lives. Some fear can be good, warning us of danger or motivating us to some greater good. However, fear is all too often our enemy. As believers we are certainly not immune to the hazards of life that often bring us to the brink of our wits, and immerse us in a brimming sea of emotions, one of which is fear. The earliest record of fear in the Bible occurs in the encounter between God and Adam and Eve. Those two, who are the parents of us all, were hiding like children after having disobeyed a parent. I can relate, can't you. Once, when I was well past my 65th birthday, my mother told some of my adult friends that I was worse than Dennis the Menace (the comic strip character) as a little boy. Although I plead the fifth against those accusations, my sister seems to remember most things as having happened just like mother said they did. While I deny those accusations, I do remember hiding when I would hear Daddy coming home from work. It seems Mother often took the approach that my mischief was best dealt with those dreaded words, "just wait until your Daddy gets home." The moment I heard his car turn in the driveway I would hide, as though somehow, I would not be found and therefore have to account for my behavior. Adam and Eve invented the strategy that I employed, hiding. God paid Adam and Eve a visit, as was the custom every day. They were not where God expected them to be, and when their whereabouts was known, God asked why they were hiding. At least they had the good sense to tell the truth. *"I was afraid."* Boom! Fear, there it is. It seems to follow us around, doesn't it? In 2 Corinthians 7:5 Paul thought so, for he said, *"we are harassed at every turn, conflicts on the outside and fears on the inside."* In Psalm 55: 4-8 is found the record of King David's struggle with fear. The Message Bible records it in this way, *"My insides are turned inside out; specters of death have me down. I shake with fear, I shudder from head to foot. Who will give me wings, I ask-wings like a dove? Get me out of here on dove wings; I want some peace and quiet. I want a walk in the country, I want a cabin in the woods. I'm desperate for a change from rage and stormy weather."*

We should also remember that David also said, *"When I am afraid, I put my trust in you. In God, whose word I praise, in God I trust, what can flesh do to me?"* (Psalm 56:3 ESV) He also said in Psalm 27:1, *"The Lord is my light and my salvation; whom shall I fear? The Lord is the stronghold of my life; of whom shall I be afraid?"* David must have experienced many fears, and he did, but he always came back to the only one who we can depend on to meet us squarely in the midst of all of our fear and follies, and the only one who can sustain us.

Judy and I found ourselves with those same emotions, often. Like the disciples in that boat we prayed and asked God, "don't you care?" That brings us back to the question, why? Why do bad things happen to good people? We were good people. Judy was a remarkable person. So, why? We asked many doctors many questions, and in return got few answers. We asked many medical researchers many questions, and in return got few answers. We even asked many, many questions of God. Over time those answers came, at least in part.

In Psalm 73:11-14 can be found the contemplation of a man named Asaph. His life is not at all going as he wished or planned. This is his attempt to get answers from God, and in verse 14, with the underpinnings of his faith beginning to crumble, he said, *"What's going on here? Is God out to lunch? Nobody's tending the store. The wicked get by with everything; they have it made, piling up riches. I've been stupid to play by the rules; what has it gotten me? A long run of bad luck, that's what—a slap in the face every time I walk out the door"* (MSG).

So, why do bad things happen to good people? First, all people, those who live commendable lives as well as those who live crude, caustic lives, experience many things just because we are all part of the human race on this earth. It is just that way. Much of what happens in our lives is beyond our control. A storm washes out the picnic you had planned for the lake. A global Pandemic shuts down your business. You find out that you have an incurable disease. The

Bible makes that very clear, "*...For he makes his sun to shine on the bad and the good, and gives rain to those who do good and to those who do evil.*" *(Matthew 5: 45 GNT)* While we have no choice in such circumstances, we do have a choice how we respond to those circumstances. Judy faced such a circumstance in her medical diagnosis. She and I prayed and prayed that God would change those circumstances, that is heal her from Alzheimer's. He is in control and all power in heaven and earth reside in Him. He could heal Judy, but He did not. That does not mean that God was angry with Judy, or that God had turned His back on her. Far from it! While God did not elect to change Judy's circumstances, God did give her the power to endure her circumstances. She lived for more than fifteen years following the Alzheimer's diagnosis. Those who knew her during those years can confirm she made a choice, a choice to keep singing, keep dancing, keep loving her family and friends and to do so with an unyielding faith that God's plan for her life was greater than anything either of us had ever imagined. How does one do that? Scripture gives us an answer, "*I know how to live on almost nothing or with everything. I have learned the secret of living in every situation, whether it is with a full stomach or empty, with plenty or little. For I can do everything through Christ, who gives me strength.*" *(Philippians 4:12-13 NLT)* So, yes, many circumstances come into lives, not because we have disobeyed God and He is angry or trying to teach us a lesson, but simply because we got into the boat when Jesus said, "*let us go to the other side.*"

While much of the suffering that comes into our lives is the result of just being a part of the human family, there is some suffering that is self- induced. The underlying cause with self-induced suffering is the misuse of our personal freedom. God created us in His image and put in us a free will, that is the ability to make choices. God is not some towering dictator, rather He is a loving God whom the Bible describes as having plans, not for evil, but for our welfare. He desires to give us a future and hope. Ever since Eden we, the creation of God, have developed strong wills determined to "do our own thing." Every choice comes with its own consequence. Wrong choices typically lead to unintended outcomes. A life spent in the compilation of wrong choices will almost certainly end in unintended, catastrophic consequences.

Other suffering comes as the result of what others do or have done. Some people are selfish, and in their lust and quest to live without boundaries they hurt others. A drunk driver crashes into a car, killing a Mom, a Dad, and their three children, but the drunk lives. A young teen, perhaps without good role models, is lured into a gang. That teen begins to experiment with drugs and soon he and a buddy try to rob a market. Shots are fired, the storekeeper does not survive, his family must now find a way to live without him. Some young adults are scared by absent or abusive parents, and now their emotional suffering is the consequence of what, not they, but others did or did not do.

Finally, some suffering is the result of the relentless attack of Satan. His presence in this world has wrecked human lives since Adam and Eve took their first steps. He is described in the Bible as the source of all lies. It was a lie in Eden that led to the expulsion of Adam and Eve from paradise. His job description is exposed in the Bible when Jesus said, *"...the thief* (reference to the devil) *comes only to steal, kill, and destroy.* (John 10:10 CSB) The Apostle Peter said, *"...be alert. Your adversary the devil is prowling around like a roaring lion, looking for someone he can devour."* (1 Peter 5:8 CSB) Evil will remain present in the world until such time that God drops the curtain of time and the devil is locked away, and ultimately destroyed. Until that time comes, suffering as the result of evil will continue to disrupt and destroy lives.

In our lives Judy and I found that Alzheimer's disease came into her life "just because." That is, just because we, like all others, live in a fallen world. Yet, we must learn to hold on. I know, you are thinking, "hold on to what?" Hold on to the promises of God. To a nation riddled with pain and suffering, the Prophet Nahum said, *"The Lord is good, a stronghold in the day of trouble, He knows those who take refuge in Him."*

PEACEFUL CALM

As we reach this part of the story it is important that we see it for what it clearly is, something of great teaching value, both realistically and symbolically. From a realistic approach we learn that Jesus has power over nature. His disciples were caught in a raging storm that was soon going to capsize their boat, and Jesus rescued them from a violent storm of nature. I believe that on at least two very distinct occasions Jesus heard my cries and prevented me from being harmed or perishing in tornadoes. However, of more importance is that we learn to trust Jesus to come to our aid when any storm comes into our path. As I sit today and write this, I cannot stop thinking about the family whose little boy, only four years of age, died in the fierce storm that tore its way across our city on Easter Sunday evening. A sunny Easter became a storm of great sorrow for them. Some seem to live in a storm of being continually shaken by fear and anxiety. In 2018 it was reported that more than 40 million American adults were being treated for anxiety. There can be found several different definitions of, and reasons given for, anxiety. The general definition given is that a person feels anxious on most days, worrying about lots of different things, and it lasts for a period of six months or more. It is estimated that U.S. expenditures for mental health in 2020 will exceed $238 billion. For Judy it was a storm of sickness, a disease for which there was no cure. Though we prayed for her healing, that healing of her body never came. For some fifteen years the disease grew worse. Her ultimate healing did come in that moment when her beautiful spirit was suddenly in the presence of Jesus, but for so many years the storm never subsided. The storms we encounter take many shapes and forms, but whatever its form, there is nothing peaceful about it.

The biblical account of the interactions of Jesus and the disciples contains four prominent facts.

First, if we look closely, we will see the promise made by Jesus. Had the disciples, who had by now seen Jesus perform miracle upon miracle, and they had heard all that he had taught in sermons, parables, and lessons, only listened carefully to the words of Jesus, there would have been no cause for fear. When Jesus expressed his intention to cross the lake, he did not make a request nor ask a question. He issued a statement which, for those paying attention, included a promise. Jesus said, *"Let us cross over to the other side."* That statement contains not a single hint of reservation, but in fact it is an affirmation...we will make it to the other side. Therein lies the promise. Every person in that boat was going to make it across the lake.

No matter the intensity of the storm, no matter the duration of the storm, they were all going to make it safely to the other side. If only the disciples had remembered those words of Jesus as their boat was filling with water...we will make to the other side. Too often I have allowed my fears and anxiety to crowd out the promises of God, and when that happens, I am only exacerbating the problem. Jesus said, *"Do not let your hearts be troubled. Trust in God; also trust me.* (John 14:1 NIV)

Secondly, there was the proclamation made by Jesus when he said, *"Peace! Be still."* The Message Bible states it, *"Quiet! Settle down."* Dr. Kenneth Wuest says that it literally means, *"Hush up and stay that way."* Nature itself had to obey the commands of the Creator. Howling winds and roaring seas obeyed the voice of Jesus. Demons fled at the name of Jesus and the sick and dying were healed by Jesus. The power of Jesus was on full display in that boat, so much so that even the disciples asked among themselves, *"Who is this, that even the wind and the sea obey him?"* Jesus Christ is the master of all our circumstances, and we can be assured that he is sufficient for any emergency that might arise.

The third, and perhaps the most pertinent fact was the very presence of Jesus. Laying fast asleep in the front of the boat was He of whom John said, *"all things were made by Him; and without Him was not anything made that was made."* (John 1:3) Creation reveals God, and Jesus was the agent of creation. What does that reveal to us? Paul provides that answer by saying, *"for since the creation of the world God's invisible qualities – his eternal power and divine nature – have been clearly seen, being understood from what has been made, so that men are without excuse."* Roman 1:20 NIV) On that day, on that lake, in that boat, Jesus was the presence and revelation of God. In that boat, along with the disciples, rode the fullness of God's glory in Jesus. May we fully appreciate the presence of God in our storms.

Finally, those men in the boat experienced the peace that Jesus brings even the midst of the storms. The enemy of peace is worry and anxiety. When sorrow and sickness try to rob us of our peace, trust Jesus. When fear and uncertainly invade our thought life, trust Jesus. When answers seem to evade us, trust Jesus. There is an old hymn that simply says, *Turn your eyes upon Jesus, look full into his wonderful face, and the things of earth will grow strangely dim in the light of His glory and grace."*

6

TREASURE IN JARS OF CLAY

Make no mistake, Judy was the greatest earthly treasure that God had ever brought into my life. Together she and I were blessed by God beyond measure, and we knew it, and we expressed our thanks to God often and in a multitude of ways. The Apostle Paul uses the expression *"treasure in jars of clay"* in 2 Corinthians 4:7 (ESV), *"But we have this treasure in jars of clay, to show that the surpassing power belongs to God, and not to us."* A treasure is something precious and priceless. Something of tremendous value. The treasure Paul spoke about was the gospel of Jesus Christ, and the power of the gospel to change lives. It is those jars of clay that captured my attention. Judy, along with all the rest of us, comprise the vast assortment of clay jars that God has collected, filled to the brim with his Spirit along with untold blessings, and uses each day to bless and minister to all those around us. Can't you just see it? My grandmother and my mother had many treasured pieces throughout their homes. In fact, I have such a treasure that was passed down to me from my mother. It is a blue flower vase that she received on the day I was born. That vase adorned her house for sixty-eight years. Now, more than seventy years after she first received the vase, it sits in my house. A seventy-two-year-old vase, that in 1949 likely cost a few dollars, resides on my dresser and it is one of my treasures that is beyond price. Its value to me is not a function of its original price, or even that it was given to my mother at my birth. Its deemed value to me is the value that my mother placed on that vase. For almost seventy years she protected it, gave it a place of prominence in her home, and valued what it represented. To anyone else I am sure it looked like any other baby blue vase, but to my mother it was anything but common. You see, that is what Paul means in this verse of scripture. Our lives, those jars of clay, may often appear common and seem mundane. Yet, they contain a treasure that is anything but common and ordinary.

Later in Paul's life, as is recorded in 2 Timothy 4:6 (ESV), he said, *"For I am ready to be poured out…."* He was referencing the fact that his life would soon end, and he once again used the imagery of a jar, and now its final contents are going to be emptied. He had been entrusted with something precious and costly and he could be assured that he had lived life well, and would hear the Master's, *"well done, my good and faithful servant…now let's celebrate together."* (Matthew 25:21 NLT) How does one get invited to that celebration?

Praise Even When

2 CORINTHIANS 1:3-7

Frankly, I had much rather spend my time around an optimistic person rather than someone who seems to see the bad side of everything. We have all met that perpetual pessimist. You know the type. Cartoonist Al Capp captured the essence of the person I am talking about in his comic strip character Joe Btfsplk, who appeared in the Li'l Abner comic strip series. Now, Joe seemed oblivious to the fact that he left a path of destruction with every step he made. Bad luck followed poor ole Joe everywhere he went. To illustrate just how bad things were for Joe, Al Capp always drew him with a black cloud hanging over his head. I have met several Joe's, and I try to avoid them if at all possible. Give me the optimist anytime! They are filled with hope and seek to see the good in most things.

However, I am not suggesting that we adopt an approach to life that is blindly optimistic, Pollyanna if you will, that could lead to self-deception and an inability to realistically judge a situation. I am recommending the approach that the Apostle Paul takes in his second letter to the church in Corinth.

Paul's approach was not blind optimism, nor was his approach based on the idea of happiness, but his approach was based on a level of joy that could not be diminished by circumstances. In this section of his letter he said, *"Blessed be the God and Father of our Lord Jesus Christ, the Father of mercies and God of all comfort, who comforts us in all our affliction, so that we may be able to comfort those who are in any affliction...."* As we soon discover in these first few chapters of Second Corinthians, Paul was no stranger to danger, dark days, discouragement, and even bouts with great despondency. And it is so God-like to not allow those emotions, as experienced by Paul, to be hidden from our purview. For if the great Apostle Paul could wrestle with those experiences and emotions, then surely, we find some measure of encouragement and even an example of how we can press on in even in dire circumstances.

Several important ideas appear in these verses of Scripture. First, there is the experience of affliction. Paul pointed to his own experiences of affliction and clearly expresses the idea that similar afflictions will come to all of us. That fact was especially true in that first century when there was often a violent reaction and resistance to Jesus Christ and the early church. On a broader scale, we have earlier noted that often bad things happen to good people just because we are all part of humanity. For Paul, much of the affliction came in the form of religious persecution, and that often violent form of persecution still exists today. The world is an imperfect place, filled with imperfect people who are capable of vile and violent acts against fellow human beings. Social injustice still rears its ugly head, while great inequities divide the haves and the have nots. Disease is not a respecter of persons regardless of race or age. Affliction and suffering are here to stay until the day of ultimate redemption when Jesus Christ returns in Kingdom power and glory.

Secondly, Paul uses the word endure to remind us that in order to survive these experiences of affliction it will require that we have the endurance of an athlete. In Hebrews 12: 1-2 (ESV) are found these words which are intended to encourage us, *"Therefore, since we are surrounded by so great a cloud of witnesses, let us also lay aside every weight, and sin which clings so closely, and let us run with endurance the race that that is set before us, looking to Jesus, the founder and perfecter of our faith…"* In my student days I both loved and played football. The entire football season is a grind, but nothing compares to the month-long preseason practices which begin in early August. In Alabama, during the month of August, the air is stale, the heat of the sun is oppressive, and the practices themselves are brutal. One does not survive without grit and endurance. But as much as I loved football, track was my favorite sport. I was a sprinter and back then we ran in events that were measured in yards, rather than measured in meters as they are now. I readily admit that while I greatly admired the feats of my track mates who were long distance runners, I never wanted to trade places with them. While I was running sprints ranging from 100 yards to 440 yards, they were running in events often measured in miles. No thanks! I did learn, as did the Apostle Paul, that no runner can expect to win any race without endurance training and ensuring that no unnecessary weight or encumbrance accompanied one onto the track. The Apostle well understood that our lives are much more akin to those long-distance races which requires great endurance and perseverance. Paul connects the word comfort to the idea of endurance. Paul refers to God as "the God of all comfort." At its root the word comfort means courage. Therefore, God is the God of all courage. Whatever form our affliction may come in, God is there to supply courage. This comfort, that is courage, is that which enables the believer to confront whatever life brings with faith and courage. In this we find the blessed assurance to run the marathon which requires of us every ounce of endurance we have, by faith, developed. The third idea here rests on Paul's words, *"Blessed be the God and Father of our Lord Jesus Christ…."* This is clearly an expression of adoration. No matter the extent of the affliction, Paul's faith rose up in him in an expression of praise for who God is and all that God had done for him, even when life brought him pain. It brings to mind the simple little song that Bill and Gloria Gaither wrote with the title that pointedly says it all: *Let's Just Praise the Lord.* Indeed, even in the most stressful and dreadful moments in our lives, if we lift our hearts and head to heaven we will find the calm and courage to praise the Lord..

As all who knew her will attest, Judy's faith was unwavering, and in so many ways the song of praise that God put in her heart remained to the end.

PRAYING THROUGH THE PAIN

Something rather remarkable comes to light in the next section of 2 Corinthians 1: 8-11. Paul says, "*...For we were so utterly burdened beyond our strength that we despaired of life itself.*" In the Good News Bible that verse reads, "*...the burdens laid upon us were so great and so heavy that we gave up all hope of staying alive.*" While it is never made clear what those circumstances were that brought Paul to the brink of despair, as we read on in the Bible we can readily see that he was never alone in his moments of peril and pain. Whether it was some form of sickness or disease that had come upon him, or the continuing harassment and bodily attacks from enemies, or even some force of Satan that tried to assault him, the Apostle is quick to affirm that it all served to remind him that he could not rely upon his own devices or knowledge to extricate himself from the great affliction. The encouragement that Paul had, and the encouragement that we have, is found in this testimony, "*...He will deliver us...we have set our hope that He will deliver us again...*"

More than causal attention should be paid to what Paul has to say about prayer in the midst of some of our most unimaginable circumstances. In verse eleven of chapter one he is speaking directly to his fellow Christians in the Corinthian church when he says, "*You also must help us by prayer, so that many will give thanks on our behalf for the blessing granted us through the prayers of many.*" Judy and I were blessed during her long illness in knowing that we had so many people praying with us and for us. Within our own church we were acquainted with several thousand people. In our Bible class at that same church we fellowshipped with and ministered to well over one hundred people. Most of my family has strong faith connections in their own places of worship. Through clients and business connections, most of whom were believers, we knew several hundred more people. Acquired across several decades, there are dozens upon dozens of my pastor and ministry friends. Judy and I knew that there were literally thousands of people who had prayed and were praying for her. The Apostle's testimony in these scriptures is that the intensity of his peril (*"we felt that we had received a sentence of death" verse 9)* had driven him closer to God, and to his knees in prayer. It is not some glib clique when we boldly declare, "there is power in prayer." Like the great Apostle, Judy and I knew that we were being sustained by the prayers of many.

PLANS CAN GO AWRY

In 1987, surrounded by stacks of papers, tax returns, and a list of all that we owed, Judy and I sat at our dining room table working on a financial plan for ourselves. We had made a list of goals that were important to us, and that we believed would honor God. As we created a written list of those goals we also thought and worked diligently to assign a monetary value and a timeframe to each goal. At the core of that financial plan were found such things as planning for the education of daughters Joy and Jennifer. We were living in a house that Judy had already purchased prior to our marriage, and we wanted to purchase a house that we could truly call home. It was also important that we plan for our eventual retirement, and for us we wanted that to include investing our money in a manner that would provide retirement income, but we also wanted to purchase a motorhome and to travel around the country in that motorhome. We each knew that statistically speaking, women in the U.S.A. tend to outlive men, so it was important to me to make provisions to ensure Judy's financial wellbeing should I die before we were financially independent. Naturally, we also wanted our plan to revolve around a philosophy of generosity in both our church and community. We prayerfully implemented our plan and for sixteen years we were on track with our goals, until.

Clearly, the Apostle Paul was planning to make a second trip to the city of Corinth. He made repeated references to his desire to see his Corinthian friends. Yet, it is imperative to not miss what he said in 1: 17-18. "do *I make my plans according to the flesh (selfish desires), ready to say yes, yes and no, no at the same time?*" Paul was responding to accusations that he said one thing and then did something else. In other words, he told the Corinthians he would come to see them, but then circumstances changed, and he was prevented from making that second trip. What should not be missed is that Paul did say in 1 Corinthians 1:7 he planned to make that second visit "*if the Lord permit.*" An eventual divine interruption came into Paul's life and his original plan for a second visit had to be aborted.

That divine interruption, that "until," came in 2003, and many of those early plans that Judy and I had prayerfully and thoughtfully made were either amended or entirely abandoned. What we discovered was that that plan became very fluid, and while pieces of the original plan remained on track for a few years, before the time of Judy's death eventually arrived very little in our lives even remotely resembled those early dreams and plans. A disease that carries a death sentence with it has a way of doing that. Whereas that 1987 plan was made with long term view that would have encompassed many years, the 2003 reality became "what do we need to do today to make it through one more day?" Plans change!

When one's life is suddenly, and often dramatically interrupted, what can be done? It is not uncommon to respond in fear, anxiety, despondency, and even despair when our life plans are detoured, or in some cases destroyed. I confess to having experienced all of those emotions, and many others as well. I can say with great certainly that none of those thoughts and emotions improved my situation, nor did they solve any problem. Perhaps the best advice that could be given any of us is that which Paul gave to the Corinthians, *"... stand firm in your faith."* Sure, religious folk throw around Bible verses and cliques all the time, as if that is some sort of magic potion to cure all our ills. But no, that is not what I mean, and it was certainly not what the Apostle had in mind. It is our faith in God's ability to supply what we need, exactly when we need it, that allows us to face each new day, in both good times and bad times. Paul explained that we have both a promise and a guarantee that God will provide us with adequate supplies, (meet all our needs) and keep us secure (put His seal on us). Neither Judy nor I could have made it through those fifteen years of plans gone awry without faith in all of God's promises.

A PRESENCE AND A PROMISE

In 2 Corinthians 4:1 – 5:9, the Apostle Paul makes some of the most remarkable and encouraging comments imaginable. Paul begins with a reference to being treated disgracefully in underhanded ways. Later, in chapter eleven he adds some detail when he states that there had been imprisonments, countless beatings, five times he was whipped with 39 lashes, he had been stoned and left for dead, he had been shipwrecked and adrift at sea, he had been robbed, gone hungry, and been left without drinking water. Add to that all the church conflicts and false accusations and one quickly sees that Paul did not lead a charmed life. What a list! Yet, in Philippians 3: 13-14 (GNB) Paul makes a great affirmation, *"...the one thing I do is to forget what is behind me and do my best to reach what is ahead. So I run straight toward the goal in order to win the prize, which is God's call through Christ Jesus to the life above."* Paul goes on to say, *"I have the strength to face all conditions by the power that Christ gives me."* (Phil. 4:13 GNB) Back in 2 Corinthians 4:6, 16 can be found wonderful words of encourage. Paul reminds his readers that he had been afflicted...but was not crushed by affliction. He had been perplexed...but not to the point of despair. He had been persecuted...but not forsaken. He had been struck down...but not destroyed. Most would conclude that Paul did not have much going for him. His life sucked! Yet, in verse 16 Paul is still able to say, *"So we do not lose heart…our inner self is being renewed day by day."*

Instead of a fatalistic approach to such opposition and adversity Paul confirms that he was not disheartened by any of those horrible things. How is that possible? For Paul it was a matter of presence. Not just any presence. Paul's inner self was being renewed by an inner presence, and we learn who that presence was when Paul said, *"…knowing that He who raised the Lord Jesus will raise us also with Jesus and bring us into His presence."* Paul knew that he had a future in the presence of the Lord, but he also understood that he had the daily presence of the Lord that was providing renewal and encouragement. Like Paul, Judy and I found comfort in His presence each day, and we had the assurance that the future was certain because of Him. Again, like Paul we could say, *"as we look not to the things that are seen, but to the unseen. For the things that are seen are transient, but the things that are unseen are eternal."*

Make no mistake, Judy and I wanted to hold on to each other and to each day. We would never be ready to give up the fight against a relentless disease, and we would never be ready to give up each other and the life we had together. Yet, we knew that when that day would eventually come, it would not be the end. It would just be the beginning. For in this section of Paul's letter he said, *"For we know that if the tent which is our earthly home is destroyed, we have a building from God, a house not made with hands, eternal in the heavens…so that what is mortal may be swallowed up by life."* After her original diagnosis, but long before the advanced stages of Alzheimer's Disease robbed her of so many cognitive abilities, Judy and I talked often about all that was encompassed in Paul's words, *"eternal in the heavens."* We took literally the words of the Apostle John in Revelation 21: 3-5, *"…God himself will be with them as their God. He will wipe away every tear from their eyes, and death shall be no more, neither shall there be mourning, nor crying, nor pain anymore, for the former things have passed away. And he who was seated on the throne said, 'behold I make all things new.' Also he said, "Write this down, for these words and trustworthy and true…."* Before her death Judy was no longer able to talk, walk, or care for herself in any manner.

Swallowing became more and more difficult. Her weight declined to about seventy pounds. It was heartbreaking....it was wretched! But in that moment her sweet spirit left that frail, impaired body behind, she was fully alive in the presence of Jesus. In her absence I am left with her memories and at times find life bearable only by the promises of scripture, which includes, *"absent from the body, present with the Lord,"* and the firm assurance that I take from Paul, *"....we are always of good courage. We know that while we are at home in the body we are away from the Lord, for we walk by faith, not by sight. Yes, we are of good courage, and we would rather be away from the body and at home with the Lord."* Yes, to paraphrase the words from *Soon and Very Soon,* an Andraé Crouch song, soon, we will see the King of Kings.

7

CAN YOU DIE FROM A BROKEN HEART?

S outhern barbeque, also known as BBQ, is both an art and a delicacy. Any Southerner worth their salt knows the difference between the various regional art forms of BBQ. North Carolina likes it vinegary, South Carolina likes it sweet, Alabamians prefer a little mayo stirred in the sauce, in Memphis it's all about dry rubbed ribs, and in Texas…well, they say everything is bigger in Texas, and so is their taste in sauces…it's more regional in that State. One thing Texans tend to agree on is that it is not real BBQ unless it is beef brisket. My Dad loved to have backyard BBQ's. He would take a fifty-five-gallon steel drum, cut it in half (long-ways), weld on some legs, place a heavy steel screen on it, and fire up the grill. My friend Darrell over in Memphis is on a highly competitive BBQ team. BBQ is a big deal to Southerners! Buster Stuart, who was my business partner for more than thirty years, and I have eaten BBQ hundreds of times at a place in Chattanooga called Rib 'n Loin. Yogi, one of my neighbors owns the place, and I smile every time I see the phone number to Rib 'n Loin…499-OINK. I personally have served their BBQ to more than a thousand people. My youngest daughter had a large outdoor wedding at an old Southern mansion, and we served BBQ from Rib 'n Loin. We once had a big party for our clients out on our office parking lot. We had games, entertainment and, you guessed it, BBQ from Rib 'n Loin. I have fed BBQ from Rib 'n Loin to my Sunday School class many, many times. Here in the South when friends die, we take food to feed the family who attend the funeral. Know what I take to them? Yup! BBQ. I love BBQ, and my favorite haunt to eat it is Rib 'n Loin.

By now there are probably two thoughts rambling around in your head. One question is, "Man, I'm really hungry for some barbeque," and the second question is, "What has this got to do with a broken heart?" The answer to the first question is, call my friend Yogi. The answer to the second question is, everything.

BROKEN HEARTS

I've heard about it and so have you. I can think of a couple of instances in which I believe that it did in fact happen. You know, it's typically an older couple in which one of them dies, and then in a relatively short period of time the other person dies as well. When such an event occurs, we might say, "I think they died of a broken heart." We say it, but can it be true? Science concludes that there could be a lot of truth in what most simply pass off as some urban legend perpetuated across the centuries. Yet, there is no denying the internal impact of stress on the human mind and body. A flood of hormones pours into our bodies in response to some traumatic event or circumstance. In particular, the stress hormones like adrenaline and cortisol begin to course through our body leaving a potential trail of damage that could lead to death. The so-called fight or flight syndrome brings about dramatic change to the chemistry of the human body. At best, one's body is given the ability to respond to the challenge in a manner often outside of one's usual capabilities. We have all heard about some person's ability to lift an automobile to save an individual from certain death. In September 2019 CNN reported an incident in which a sixteen-year old boy, living in Butler, Ohio, lifted a car that had fallen off its jack and had the boy's neighbor pinned under it. The man's wife was hysterical (who wouldn't be?) and the boy and his mother, who were in their yard, heard the commotion. The young man was able to lift the car long enough for the man's wife and the boy's mother to pull him from under the car. It is that sudden, uncharacteristic, burst of strength, speed and presence of mind that comes from that flood of hormones. At its worst, the same flood of chemicals that can bring about that burst of strength and energy can also put the heart under attack. In fact, it can lead to a heart attack. The extended presence of those hormones raises blood pressure, constricts blood vessels, effects the digestive system, increases the propensity for blood clots, faulty heart rhythms, and if perpetuated can lead to cardiac arrest. Harvard Medical School reports that there is a growing consensus among scientists that what was once considered an old wives' tale is likely true: Yes, we can die from a broken heart. Grief can kill us.

WHO CARES?

Who cares for the millions of known cases of Alzheimer's in the United States? In 2019, caregivers of people with Alzheimer's and other forms of dementia provided an estimated 18.6 billion hours of unpaid care. It should not be overlooked that those hours serving family members and friends is estimated to have a value of $244 billion. Think about that! In very real terms that is a $244 billion contribution to our nation. Staggering numbers, indeed! Total payments in 2020 for all individuals with Alzheimer's and other forms of dementia are estimated to reach $305 billion – not including unpaid caregiving. In 2019 the total lifetime cost for caring for someone with dementia was approximately $357,000.00 – not accounting for future inflation. Whereas we have in 2020 five million diagnosed cases of Alzheimer's, it is highly likely that many more go undiagnosed. The number of cases is expected to triple by 2050 and with that rise in cases, the projected increase in the total payments for health care, long-term care and hospice care is estimated to rise to $1.1 trillion.

Not counting the cost of paid caregiving, there are many other expenses to consider. Medicines, participation in experimental treatments, and various forms of testing, special needs items not covered by major medical insurance plans are just a few examples. Judy volunteered for certain clinical trials, one of which was being done at a major research and teaching hospital in New York. It involved a twice monthly infusion for one year, with each infusion taking about two hours. Clinical trials typically have no cost for participation. However, this one was in New York which meant that we would need to travel there, during the course of the trial, twenty-four times. Judy's doctor was optimistic about this trial – and so were we, but we had no idea how we would pull off all those trips. Her doctor persuaded the clinical researcher to allow her to participate in Chattanooga without those trips to New York. She and I were both elated, for it meant that we knew that she was not going to be receiving a placebo, but she would actually be receiving the trial drug. Their willingness did not come without a price. The clinical trial included testing at the end of each month during the twelve-month period to determine what, if anything, was changing. Six months into the trial Judy's scores were continuing to dramatically decline. The doctor told us, based on the fact we had paid $22,800.00 for six months of participation, that Judy should withdraw from the study. Not counting the caregiving provided by us, her family, the cost of paid caregiving for Judy exceeded

$440,000.00. Prudent planning on our part, to include Long Term Care insurance in our financial plan, meant that the great majority of that amount was paid by the insurance company.

So, who cares? We must all care, for if the statistical data is correct, and we do see a tripling of Alzheimer's diagnoses and the attendant escalating costs of that increase, it has the potential to be a tidal wave of financial shock to both personal and national checkbooks.

A GIFT FOR JUDY

My plan of care for Judy had always been that I, along with any help needed, would care for her in our home. By 2006 I no longer felt comfortable leaving Judy at home all day while I worked. She was still capable of taking care of her personal grooming needs and simple tasks around the house. My mother, who lived nearby, came by to check on Judy, and spent several hours during each weekday with Judy. They would lunch together, go shopping and generally do about anything they chose to do. What a blessing my mother was to Judy in those early years of Judy's battle with Alzheimer's. Early in our marriage Judy and Mother had formed an amazing bond. Judy's mother lived with us for a long, long time, and during that time my mother and Judy's mother were great friends. Mom and Judy both had sweet dispositions and I found such comfort in their relationship. Mother's care for Judy continued for many years, and naturally the level of care Judy needed continued to rise. Having observed numerous situations in which home care for a family member was both trying and vexing, I was richly blessed to have the gift of my mother to spend so much time with Judy.

Judy's experience with Alzheimer's did not follow the textbooks. She far outlived the so-called life expectancy for both early-onset Alzheimer's and the disease in general. The literature on the disease discusses the various stages for Alzheimer's, but in so many ways Judy's experience was not always compatible with those ideas. That is not to say that knowing that information is not helpful, because we did find in helpful, and in some ways found encouragement that

Judy's passage with the disease was different, and different in a positive way. Neither Judy nor I dabbled much with the issue of denial. Rather, we spent those early years planning for what the future could bring our way, but equally, if not more important, was our shared determination to live our lives to the fullest extent possible. We re-entrenched ourselves in our faith, we refreshed our financial plans, and we revisited our estate plans. With the estate plans our wills needed no amendments, but we worked with our attorney to ensure that our health care directives and our living wills were clearly in line with our wishes. Our durable Power of Attorney documents needed no revisions. Having done that…we lived! Our goal was to wring from each day, month, and year as much as humanly possible within the allotted time that God was giving us.

By 2010 Judy needed much more care. My mother was such a caring, loving rock in Judy's life. Mother was now spending at least six hours per day, five days per week, with Judy. I would relieve her immediately after leaving the office, and of course I spent the weekends caring for Judy. By this time Judy needed assistance dressing, bathing, and eating. With time the list of her needs grew, and we were again blessed to find additional help. Charlotte, the mother-in-law of our daughter Joy, became a caregiver for Judy, and she and my mother alternated days, and I was, of course, with Judy evenings and weekends. One of my fondest memories is of walking through the door, rounding the corner, and saying, "there is my girl." Judy's eyes would widen, her lips would curl into a smile and she would try to stand up from her chair. That moment each afternoon, was the highlight of my day for so long.

A long series of surgeries plagued my mother through 2013 and into 2014. Charlotte, like Mom, was a loving friend for Judy, and she repeatedly demonstrated that love. Judy returned that love and I am forever thankful for Charlotte's presence in our lives, both before and during Alzheimer's.

EVERYTHING CHANGED

Humidity was off the charts and the summer Southern heat at high noon could "take your breath away." My long-time business partner Buster and I had poked around the office all morning waiting on technicians to complete the transition of our local computer network to a new server in Minneapolis. The work was proving more tedious than we had expected, and we were unable to be very productive without the computers. Worry and exasperation caught up with us and we were soon on our way to lunch, assuring ourselves that the work would be completed by the time we returned.

Sometimes you can see the heat rising off the asphalt. Our walk into the restaurant was a bit brisker today as we anticipated getting out of the heat, and into Yogi's, which he always kept cold enough to "hang meat." Buster and I ate lunch several times each week at the Rib 'n Loin barbeque restaurant, so much so that all the employees all knew us by name. Brenda, our server, had simply asked, "your usual?" Soon the iced teas were on the table and would quickly be followed by the real food. Then something happened. When I told Buster that I was not feeling well he naturally asked what might be wrong. My reply was, "my jaw hurts, as well as my neck and shoulder, and my left arm hurts too." He stood and walked away and returned from the check-out with a bottle of aspirin. After some urging and conversation about a potential heart attack, I took not one aspirin, but four. By the time our food arrived I was handing the keys to my car to Buster and we were walking out the door on the way to the hospital. That was on Tuesday, August 14, 2014. I left that hospital on August 21, after having not only a heart attack, but five coronary bypasses. I would not return to work part-time until October, but that was the least of my concerns. That trip to the Rib 'n Loin had changed everything…and I never even ate that lunch!

IT'S ALL ABOUT JUDY

Admittedly, my recovery went very well. I left the hospital with a powerful pain killer, only one of which I ever took. My greatest battle, on the recommendation of the doctor, was trying to sleep in a recliner. I just could not fall asleep. Thinking it might put me to sleep, I took one of those pain pills. Wrong…worst night ever! Other than that experience, my needs were few. After all, my Sunday School class brought lunch and dinner every day for thirty days. Truly, my needs were minimal.

Charlotte had been so very gracious in remaining with Judy during my hospitalization. Mother was confined to her home continuing her recovery, and in fact home health staff was going into her home to assist her. Our dilemma lay around Judy's need for "round-the-clock" care, and Charlotte was more than willing to continue coming each day, but she could not be expected to be constantly available. We reached out to an old friend who was a retired nurse, and she quickly assembled a team of her friends who were personal caregivers. Now we had Charlotte for weekdays and two caregivers for weeknights. There was also a two-person team who came into our home and provided weekend care for Judy. They were all marvelous, and I was of course still confined to the house, but most importantly, Judy's needs were being met.

By late September I was allowed to drive, and my driving primarily consisted of driving to my three times per week cardiac rehab sessions. I drove with a pillow between my chest and the steering wheel of my car for several weeks. Early October brought a limited work schedule, and the staff of full- time caregivers continued to do an excellent job in providing for Judy's every need. It was easy to see that all of them had quickly grown to love Judy, and Judy responded well to them.

The chill of November meant that the outdoor season was changing and that Thanksgiving was at hand, and it also meant that the restriction that had been placed on me relative to the amount of weight I could lift was soon to return to normal. That would mean a new season inside our home, because it would allow me to once again be able to lift Judy, which was necessary when she needed to move from a chair, the bed, or even into the shower. The new season also meant that I could begin to transition back into being Judy's evening and weekend caregiver. By early December we returned to the pre-surgery schedule of Charlotte caring for Judy during the day and I would return home to care for her as soon the office closed. Thanksgiving and Christmas came and went with Charlotte and me as caregivers, but something had changed, and not for the better.

SLEEPLESS IN CHATTANOOGA

The opening line to a song sung by The 5th Dimension says, *"Last night I didn't get to sleep at all…"* Judy and I had always been somewhat of a night owl. We rarely even thought about going to bed before 11:30 p.m., and while it was just the two of us at home in the evenings, that had not changed. For the period of time we had twenty-four hour per day caregivers in our house I insisted that they not put her into bed before eleven each evening. It was working, and I was convinced that it enabled Judy to sleep later the next morning, and she would typically sleep until about 9:00 a.m. each morning. So, I fell back into that pattern and would help her into bed shortly after eleven, and I would then read or tidy up the house, and then slide into bed around midnight. Suddenly, and never later than 2:00 a.m., Judy was awake and could not be coaxed to stay in the bed and try to sleep. The remedy became that I would take her into our living room, sit her in her favorite chair, and turn on some music. I had downloaded all her favorites onto an iPod, which I had connected to a somewhat sophisticated system that produced a great sound. While she sat contented, rocking in her chair to the music, I would try to sleep on the sofa. While I might drift off for brief stints, one could certainly never call it sleep. On rare occasions I might convince Judy to go back to bed, but usually she chose to remain in her chair. Charlotte would arrive by 8:30 each morning and off to the office I would go, returning home in the afternoon to repeat the past evening's down, then up schedule. Adjusting bedtime did nothing to change Judy's new habit, referred in Alzheimer's literature as "sundowning."

Searching for a solution became mind numbing. Bringing my twenty-four hour per day team of caregivers back into our home was my first solution, and I did inquire about it and the retired nurse had moved to Florida and the others already had new positions. Too many families had told me their horror stories of utilizing some of the sitting and caregiving providers. That is the least appealing of all possible in-home solutions, to me at least. It seems to be a revolving door of who is sent to your home, and it is rather expensive. The unfortunate part of that expense is that the worker is paid only $8.00 to $12.00 of what is charged, and the total charge currently ranges between $20.00 to $25.00 per hour. For me, the untenable piece was never being sure who was going to show up to spend the night in our house. I was about six months beyond my 65th birthday and entertained thoughts about retiring, yet our uncertain future, and an exit plan from our business that was still at least three years away, did not make retirement a comfortable choice. But after forty plus days of little rest and even less sleep, something had to change.

AN EDUCATION I NEVER WANTED

Beginning in February 2015 I began a forty-three-month long education in the long-term care business. I investigated and visited "group home care" facilities, assisted living facilities, and nursing homes. Since Judy and I both had "long term care" insurance it was imperative that we determine what types of care would or would not be covered by our policies. Most important of all, we needed to know which type facility could best meet Judy's needs.

Nursing homes were quickly marked off my list. The typical ratio of workers to residents quickly told me that Judy could never receive the attention I knew that I wanted her to have on a daily basis. By definition, a nursing home is for someone who needs intermediate (advanced custodial) or skilled care (doctors immediately available and supervising the staff). The definition alone seemed to indicate that Judy did not need a nursing home. She needed help with her daily needs, and someone to assist with meals, and of course to ensure her medications were taken appropriately. As I visited the typically loosely-licensed group homes I was not impressed. Besides, our local newspapers had carried more than a few group homes stories that involved both neglect and abuse. Check and check–both the group homes and the nursing homes were off my list. On to check out the assisted living options.

Our city is fortunate to have several nice, cosmetically appealing, assisted living options, and I began to visit them one by one. Since, through Rotary, I had met the owner of a chain of upscale assisted living facilities, I started there. An appointment was made with the admissions counselor and I approached that meeting with a bit of optimism, after all, I had some limited experience of visiting a few of their facilities on ministry visits. Shortly into my conversation with the admissions counselor I learned something that would become a part of my caregiving vocabulary for as long as Judy lived. Mobility. Judy could not walk without assistance, nor could she lift herself from a sitting position and stand alone. The State of Tennessee has a somewhat restrictive definition of mobility and I quickly learned that Judy's abilities and that definition would never be compatible. According to the Tennessee Standards for Assisted-Living Facilities, "ambulatory means the resident's ability to bear weight, pivot and walk safely with the use of a cane, walker, or other mechanical supportive device with or without the minimal assistance of another person. The resident must be physically and mentally capable of self-preservation by evacuating in response to an emergency. A residence who requires a wheelchair must be capable of transferring to and propelling the wheelchair independently." In no way could Judy qualify for admission to the licensed assisted-living facilities, even though in my visits to those facilities I repeatedly saw residents who could not have possibly met those standards.

One might imagine my surprise when a large, well regarded, Jesuit facility told me that Judy could be admitted to their specialized memory care—assisted living facility. I fully disclosed all of Judy's limitations, they came to our home and did an in-home evaluation of Judy and stated once again that she met the criteria. Naturally, I inquired as to how that was possible when I had been repeatedly told that Tennessee regulations for assisted living facilities rendered her ineligible. Every assurance was given to me that because this facility, named "The Valley Residence," was registered as a "Home for the Aging" the regulations made allowances for individuals with Judy's disabilities. I should have read the fine print.

Intellectually I was prepared. My analytical nature had done in depth research and reached logical conclusions. Furnishings had been purchased and my daughters helped me decorate what was to become Judy's room in the memory care facility. They also helped me organize and move into her room the clothes and personal items she would be needing. A move in date for Judy's arrival was set.

AN UNRESOLVED CONFLICT

However, one problem remained. One, really, really big problem. The one thing that I had not prepared was my heart…my emotions. There she sat, all pretty and dressed up, rocking away in her favorite chair. Contented by the music and smiling at me every time I called her by name. So sweet, so innocent, so completely unaware of what was taking place. My mind was racing and my heart pounding as we pulled up to the front door of the assisted living facility. "What have I done? I can't do this." Even as I was rolling Judy toward the front door, my heart was breaking, my mind was jumbled with thoughts of all that might go wrong. Would she be safe? Would she even understand? What if something awful happens to her? As we approached, the door opened and we were met by friendly enough staff who announced that they had been expecting us, and they then led us down a hallway, through a locked door that led into a "community room" and on into Judy's room. Judy may have not understood what was happening, but I did. "Why did I ever think this was a good idea? I can't leave her here." Administration staff had told me that it was their policy that family does not return to visit their family member for at least two weeks, supposedly giving the staff and the "new" resident a period of adjustment. There was no way on planet earth that I was going to abide by any such rules, and I told them so. I fed her lunch, and slipped out the door, knowing I would return in a few hours for her dinner. It still felt as if I were deserting her. It is hard to describe what I felt...heartbroken, a dark sadness, grief...none of the losses incurred in my life had seemed to reach this deep into my soul. What kind of horrible person could do such a thing? Can you die of a broken heart? On that day I certainly thought so....and on that day I thought I would.

I did not yet know it, but it would get worse.

8

DOES ANYBODY CARE?

The photo of the little guy immediately caught my eye and my heart. The story behind the photograph brought me to tears. His story certainly caught the attention of a few other folks, including gospel vocal artist James Gary Puckett. The core of the true story captured in a song titled *"The Backpack Song,"* is about a little third grade boy, who on a Friday at the end of a school week did not want to leave school. Now, I don't about you, but all through grammar school, high school, college and graduate schools, I cannot remember a single day that I was not thrilled when that day ended, and I could go home. However, I knew that when I arrived at home it would not be too long before supper would be on the table. The essence of that song is about that little boy who would be going home only to be hungry until he could get back to school on Monday. That thought led me to discover that one in every eight children in America goes to bed

hungry every night. How can that be? This is America for goodness sake! I'm haunted by the refrain in Puckett's song *"Does anybody care?"* Sadly, I'm convinced that there is an awful lot of awfulness in the world, and yes, right here in America, that we loudly protest and say we care…but our words are not backed up by our actions.

Does anybody care? What a question. My journey alongside Judy persuaded me that we talk a lot about caring, we write a lot about caring, but not much changes, especially when it comes to health issues that have tended to be primarily the concern of the aging and the elderly. Politicians pontificate about how much they care, corporations spend millions on facilities that are advertised as a means to care for the aging and the elderly. But I've been on the inside of the Capitol Building in Washington pleading with Congressmen and Senators to help find more funding for cures, only to be patronized and politely shown the door. I have walked the halls of those facilities, and have seen the good, the bad, and the ugly. Can you hear it…that question, does anybody care? It just never seems to go away, and I'm still looking for the answer.

The staff at the "Valley Residence" memory care facility was accommodating and friendly, and from all my hours spent there I believed they were doing a commendable job. However, I learned that an observation I had made in my years of ministry visits to long term care facilities, was in fact true. There are never enough "hands on deck" to care for the ever-occurring needs of that many people. The pay is low, the work is difficult, the hours are often long, and the turnover rate is high. Having said that, it was quickly obvious to me that Judy was not going to get the attention that I believed she needed and was accustomed to having at home. She could not talk, so she never screamed out. She couldn't walk, so she was never going to wander or become a pest to other residents. She could not feed herself, and I noticed quickly that because she was silent, she tended to be placed on the end of the feeding list. The loud, the demanding and the belligerent got the most attention. The time demand on so few workers was never more apparent than at mealtime. Those like Judy, who could not feed themselves, had to be fed by one of the workers who likely had to feed not only Judy but six or even more residents. Add to that the time element – typically thirty minutes allotted to a meal – and you can surely see where this is going. Judy, at this point in her journey, still ate very well. However, it could take thirty to forty minutes to feed her a meal. The same was true of other residents. The outcome was simple, if they can't be fed quickly, move on and record in the chart that she/he was not very hungry.

Once, after Judy was residing at a different facility, I was going to be late getting away from the office and had called ahead and asked them to begin feeding Judy. When I arrived, at least thirty plus minutes later than I normally would have, I saw Judy sitting alone, with her food tray. There were a few drops of food on her bib, but mostly, the food was uneaten. I asked, and was told, that one of the CNA's had attempted to feed Judy, but that Judy seemed disinterested in eating. I was fuming, but "bit my tongue," for the moment. I took the food tray, warmed in the microwave, then sat down with Judy...about thirty minutes later she had eaten every morsel of the food.

Meal-time issues were resolved early on for Judy's sake. Charlotte, who had helped with Judy's care at home agreed to go at lunch each weekday and feed Judy, and I then fed her dinner each evening, as well as her lunch and dinner on the weekends. I reasoned that if Judy had the opportunity for a peaceful (meaning given ample time to eat) lunch and dinner, at least those two meals would be good nourishment, and breakfast would be whatever the facility could and would do.

Valley Residence housed only those who had Alzheimer's or some other form of dementia. There were a few concerns in the first couple of weeks, but for the most part things settled into a routine. I had set up Judy's room with her favorite chair, that both rocked and swiveled, and naturally, I made arrangements with the cable TV service to ensure that Judy's TV would receive all the music channels, including of course, the sixties classics. I set the TV on that channel and dared anyone to change the channel. Judy would sit and hum and smile to the music as she used her feet to move the swivel chair from side to side. Judy and I would have dinner together and then sit in her room and listen to music, and while I don't know how much she understood of all that we "talked" about, I do know that every time I called her name, her eyes would widen, and that big beautiful smile would come across her face. More times than not, she would then lean across the arm of her chair toward me. That was the signal for a kiss. Goodness...how, I miss those kisses.

One February evening, as Judy and I sat listening to music, I caught a glimpse through the window blinds, and captured in the illumination of the streetlamp, a heavy snow was falling. I had planned to stay later, but it was already around 8:00 p.m., and I had about a twenty-mile drive to get home and had to drive across the river bridge. Chattanooga gets some snowfall most years, but that was a humdinger. By the time morning came I actually had to shovel my driveway in order to get my car out of the garage. By lunch time I had managed to make my way back to see Judy. I adopted the mantra of the Postman when it came to Judy…neither snow nor rain nor gloom of night…well, you get the idea.

Another incident, from those first two weeks, came in the form of a phone call. I had left Judy and arrived home about 9:00 p.m. and was plundering around in the kitchen for a quick dinner meal. The television was on and as the phone rang the incoming phone number rolled across the screen of the television. I recognized it immediately, it was the Valley Residence.

Judy had rolled out of the bed, and while they told me that she appeared to have no injuries she was crying inconsolably. I was suddenly walking out to my car and ending my call with the CNA in what now seems one fluid motion. I immediately phoned my daughter Jennifer, who was at least fifteen minutes closer to Judy than I was, and as I explained what was happening, she was out the door and on her way. By the time I reached the parking lot of the Valley Residence I could see that Jennifer's car was already parked there, and that immediately brought some sense of comfort to me… at least someone was in there with Judy who really cared. While I am sure it was not actually a long, long time—it seemed hours to me —before someone came to the main entrance to let me in the building. Then there was the keypad for the door leading into Judy's section of the building that seemed to be just asking for me to rip it off the wall. I am sure it was my level of anxiety that caused me to fumble with the door code, but all I cared about was seeing Judy. The nurse finally punched in the code and the door opened. As I raced toward Judy's room, I heard no commotion or crying, in fact the entire wing seemed deathly quiet. Stepping into her room I was stopped in my tracks by the scene in that room. I cried like a baby. Jennifer was sitting quietly in Judy's chair. Sitting up in the bed was Maggie, our granddaughter, who had Judy cradled in her lap. Judy was curled up, and sound asleep, like a little child in their mama's lap. Jennifer told me that Judy was still very upset when they arrived, but she had responded to Jennifer's voice, and then when she got into the bed with Maggie's arms wrapped around her she was immediately calm and quickly drifted off to sleep. Jennifer and Maggie left, and I stayed until about 1:00 a.m. Judy never moved once she was asleep. Jennifer and Maggie had been just the thing Judy needed that evening. By the time I arrived the next morning it was as though nothing had happened.

We were to soon learn that Judy's days at the Valley Residence were numbered.

I had been adamant when I discussed, with the Director of the facility, the possibility of Judy's admission to the Valley Residence. I had learned from discussions with other assistant living facilities that Judy's lack of mobility would preclude her from being admitted under Tennessee guidelines for assisted living facilities. The director made every assurance to me that their licensing was different, and it was. However, I was never told that the license which Valley Residence also included similar restrictions for those with impaired mobility. I was repeatedly told that Judy would never have to leave, and I believed them, for I saw at least five other residents in the wing in which Judy was to be housed who had similar impairments. But, without notice that director was suddenly gone and within a few days I was being told that Judy would not be allowed to remain at the Valley Residence. It had been no more than six weeks since I had agonizingly brought Judy to the facility, and now I was being told that I had two weeks to make other plans.

I can assure you – at that moment it felt like no one cared.

A GOD IDEA

I spent a frantic week following up on leads and exploring options. By this time the team of care givers I had been using for in home care had either already taken other assignments or moved to distant towns. On a Friday afternoon, after all the staff had left the office for the weekend, my business partner Buster Stuart and I were discussing my angst regarding Judy's care. It was then, though neither of us knew it at the time, Buster had a "God idea." He and his wife were planning to have dinner on Saturday evening with some friends, and the man, who was now retired, had spent his entire career in the long-term care business. Buster said that he would explain the issue with Judy's care and see what he might be able to suggest. It was through Buster's idea that God showed up with an answer. The son of Buster's friend was a senior level leader in a Georgia-based company that owned and operated Assisted Living and Memory Care facilities across the Southeast, and he would be calling me on Monday morning. His call and conversation probably lasted less than fifteen minutes and he told me that the director of the Rosewood Assisted Living center in Fort Oglethorpe, Georgia would call me before the end of the business day, and that he was certain they could help find a solution for Judy's care.

Indeed, God put all those people in my path at exactly the right time. Rosewood, although in Georgia, was much, much closer to my home than the Valley Residence. The State of Georgia regulations were much different from the Tennessee regulations, and an apartment was available for Judy. It had a bedroom, a small dining space and a living room. With the help of Joy and Jennifer, we were able to make it look and feel more like a home.

Rosewood was not without a few problems. The most significant issue, like most of the facilities in that industry, was the lack of staff. While certainly not unique to them, there was always a lot of turnover, and especially on weekends, never enough staff. The memory care section was blessed to have a lead nurse who genuinely cared, and even loved, those residents. It showed up in her words and her work. The only issue that they could never seem to solve in the memory care unit was the food service. While I never cared for some of their combinations, the major issue was quantity. I once took a photo of a dinner plate they brought in for Judy and sent the photo to the administrator. The amount of food on the plate was not even adequate for a small child. I am convinced that the administrator addressed my concern with the food staff, but any change that came about was short lived. My solution for that was to stop every afternoon on my way to feed Judy and pick up food to complement what was on the menu for that particular day. The Rosewood staff quickly learned that my presence, or in my absence the presence of someone else representing me, was going to be a constant. I felt that Judy needed and deserved an advocate and a voice, and I was qualified for that job.

One winter the entire facility was quarantined by the County Health Department because the Norovirus made its ugly appearance in Rosewood. It began in the assisted living section and quickly made its way into the memory care section. Judy, like all other residents and many staff members, was infected. It was strongly recommended that I stay away, but that was not going to happen. I followed their protocol while in the building, but I was not going to not see Judy. Had Judy been alive during this so-called pandemic I would have moved her home.

One of the best things that happened while at Rosewood took place when a nurse, who had been in to see Judy, called me aside and asked me if I had ever considered using Hospice to help me with Judy. No doubt, seeing the gasp in my expression, she quickly explained that she was in no way saying Judy's condition was suddenly worse and that death was imminent. She explained that Judy's Alzheimer's diagnosis met the definition for additional services from any hospice organization. I learned that they could provide services not just for weeks or months, but even for years, if the diagnosis says there is no reasonable expectation for recovery. Alzheimer's, sadly, still has zero expectation for recovery. Judy was assigned a wonderful team of seemingly caring people. Her registered nurse from hospice gave me her cell phone number and she made routine calls to let me know how her visits to see Judy had gone. Judy, like a lot of long-term care residents, developed a propensity for urinary tract infections. I knew when she had a UTI. It changed her behavior, she could not sit still, and there was physical evidence as well. The Rosewood staff always addressed it, but lab results often took days, and even then, the attending physician had to order the medicine which would be delivered one or two days later from a distant contract pharmacy. In exasperation, I once took a prescription that was going to "lay around" the facility over the weekend until it could be transmitted to the contract pharmacy on Monday, and went directly to a local pharmacy and had it filled. I knew Judy was in misery because of the UTI and I could not bear the thought of her not getting meds for another two or three days. That became one immediate benefit of the hospice nurse. She had the ability to get those basic antibiotics when needed. I never had reason to regret my decision, in fact I am certain that they added another level of care to the care of the nurses and aids in the memory care unit. My Judy now had lots of eyes and hands available to her.

Other than minor annoyances—other residents wandered around in Judy's room—I have found them asleep in her bed, on the sofa—residents taking Judy's personal items and even clothes—I found ways to cope and address Judy's ever changing needs as well as the changing dynamics of Rosewood.

Beginning in about the thirtieth month of Judy's stay there I could sense that something was shifting. There were more visits from state inspectors. Some of the devices that I had in Judy's room, all of which I placed there for her safety, were suddenly being deemed outside the bounds of state guidelines. It became so ridiculous that inspectors and regulators said that residents could no longer have a food tray attached to the front of their "geriatric chair." I watched in stunned amazement as the aides and nurses now had to push those chairs, minus the food tray, up to the dining tables at mealtime. That left the resident sitting more than two feet from the table and their food. By the end of the meal, most of their food and beverage was in their lap rather than their stomach. The "older" inspectors had been replaced with young adults who likely had just graduated with their social work degree and had been given a state manual; most of them had little to no knowledge of "real life" (by the way, this is an opinion, but one based on observation of how institutionalized agencies can work). Bit by bit, they whittled away—then by Judy's thirty second month there—someone had supposedly pressed the agencies, who in turn pressed the legislators—to amend the operational guidelines in Georgia for assisted living and memory care facilities. Yes, we are moving again. Does anybody care?

In terms of appearances, Lifecare Center of East Ridge is the Taj Mahal of nursing homes. Judy's continual decline, physically and mentally, has brought me to the front door of what I never believed I would be doing. From that day I first drove her to Valley Residence, my frequent companion has been an overwhelming sadness. The beautiful and wonderful woman that I love likely did not really know who I was. She could do nothing to care for herself. Though I spent a great deal of my time with her, I still had to leave her behind every night, and I returned to a dark, empty house, a place which long ago stopped being a home. It had become little more than a place to sleep.

Lifecare of East Ridge is by license a nursing home for long term care, and a rehabilitation center. In mid-February 2018 Judy became their first resident for long term care. All other residents were in rehab, and since Medicare pays for ninety days of rehab, the turnover was constant. Judy was the first, and remained the only, long term resident for the seven plus months she remained there.

The experience at Lifecare, for the most part, was accommodating. The food was very good, and there was a beautiful dining room, complete with linen tablecloths and napkins. While Judy remained in her room for most meals, on Sundays, when Judy was having a good day, I would take her to the dining room for the noon meal. Also, on Sunday afternoons, they had an ice cream shop and with Judy in her specially equipped wheelchair, we could venture over to the ice cream shop. Her favorite had always been, and seemed to remain, chocolate and mine was always either strawberry or butter pecan. Most of the time we ate our ice cream at one of the inside tables, but on occasion I would push Judy outside into the courtyard where we would devour our frozen treats.

For Judy's entire stay in the Valley Residence, Rosewood, and Lifecare I made certain that her lunch and dinner was fed to her by either Charlotte or myself. On those rare instances when Charlotte was not available another family member, or one of our friends would step in to ensure that someone was there to be certain Judy had the opportunity to eat her meal, and at her pace.

While a beautiful facility, Lifecare of East Ridge had some of the same shortcomings as our other experiences, primarily too many patients for the staff. I observed, especially in Judy's section, that CNA's were in short supply and I too often found Judy either not being toileted often enough, and I dreaded weekends, because it often meant nursing staff being "borrowed" from other Lifecare locations to cover the weekend. I can say that I never found them very engaged or engaging. I once became irate with one such nurse because she was ranked near the top of the list of either the most incompetent, or uncaring, persons I had ever met. I knew that Judy once again had a UTI and I had asked the staff on a Thursday to get a sample tested. It was late on Friday, when I did it myself, that the sample was collected. I made certain that it was forwarded on to the lab and I was told that even though it was going into the weekend that the result would be faxed back to the nursing station on Judy's hall by noon on Saturday. When noon rolled around I was standing at the counter of the nursing station asking if they had received the report. The nurse was someone I had never seen before, and without looking up in my direction she mumbled something and said, "I haven't seen it." My thought, which went unsaid, was I guess you haven't seen it, because I have not seen you move out of that chair all morning. I left that thought unsaid, but I did tell her that I would return in about half an hour to check again. That little "dance" continued until almost 4:00 p.m., at which time I went around the counter, over her objection of "you can't come back here," into the space that served as the nurses' office for that section of the facility. I knew the fax machine was in that office and I went directly to it and quickly thumbed through a stack of papers lying next to the fax machine. There it was! Time stamped at 12:27 p.m. EST. Furthermore, the report indicated that Judy did in fact have the UTI issue again. I was livid and marched off to another section of the building and found the nurse for that section. I explained what had happened and she took the report and told me that she would contact the attending physician. Even though 4:00 p.m. was the daily final delivery of medicine from the contract pharmacy it was dispatched and delivered by about 8:00 p.m. Had I stood around waiting on the uncaring attitude of the "borrowed" nurse, that lab report would have not even been read until the following Monday, and Judy would have remained in misery. It is important to note that at that point in time Lifecare did not allow any hospice agencies in that facility. That was later amended, but in the eight months of her stay at Lifecare Judy had no access to hospice. Had it been available, I would have certainly brought them alongside the Lifecare staff to ensure that Judy had the additional assistance I then believed, and still believe, she needed. Judy did have hospice care the final three days of her life.

On Monday morning I made a visit to the administrator's office and filed a complaint. He told me he would investigate who the person was, and where she was assigned. I calmly replied that the who or where was of little concern to me, that I only wanted to ensure that she was never allowed to be near Judy again. The next day, as I was on my way to Judy's room, the administrator saw me in the hallway and told me he had followed up on my concerns and that that person would not be back in the facility he managed. Thankfully, I can say that I never saw that nurse again.

My point of emphasis is simple, if someone you love and cherish is confined to any type facility—short or long term—make sure you are seen and heard regularly, and the more the better. Judy was in either assisted living facilities or a nursing home for the last forty-two months of her life. There was not a single day that there was not someone, either family or friends, who checked on her at multiple points during the day, and right up until bedtime. I saw first-hand the difference regular family presence makes in terms of resident care and attention.

Lifecare of Eastridge was Judy's home for slightly over seven months. Her decline had become steady. Her weight had dropped to less than seventy-five pounds. The staff developed a routine of giving her protein shakes—chocolate of course—in an attempt to stem the weight loss.

The first day of Fall 2018 had just come and gone, and I was worried.

Does anybody care?

9

GOODNIGHT SWEETHEART,
GOODNIGHT

Happy-ever-after endings are the stuff of fairytales and Hallmark movies. Almost sixteen years after Judy and I sat tearfully wincing and grim faced in Dr. Kodsi's office, it was increasingly clear that our love story would not end with rose petals and dancing in the streets. As the years passed, and especially the first nine months of 2018, it was increasingly obvious that the speed at which the disease was progressing was much more rapid than at any point in the entire span of these now many years. Grieving and tears had long been my companion. There had been so many self-directed pep talks. Up until her death the previous year I had the never ending, ever present prayers and encouragement of my elderly mother. Our children, grandchildren, church friends and so many wonderful, supportive, people had been around us for the entire journey. I will be ever grateful for all those wonderful people, yet each night that I went home after spending the evening with Judy, the house felt as though I was walking into a dark abyss. In Nevada, up along the Oregon border, there exists what is described as "an immense area of darkness." That corner of Nevada is considered one the darkest places on earth. Absent Judy's presence, I contend that that house I walked into every night was the darkest place on earth. Summer passed into the Fall, and although I did not know it, it was about to get even darker.

HERE AND NOW - THEN AND THERE

I convinced myself that I was prepared for the inevitable. I was not! Philosophically, perhaps. Theologically, sure. Emotionally, no! Around 7:40 a.m. on a Saturday morning Judy's spirit flew across the great divide of the here and now and the then and there. She is free from that wretched disease that stole her from me, from all of us, bit by bit. She was gloriously, as the Apostle Paul called it, *"in the twinkling of an eye,"* moved out of the jar of clay that was her body and moved into the presence of the Lord. For that I rejoice. However, I was left with a punch in the gut, a hole in my heart, and stuck in the here and now while loving and longing for my dear Judy who had moved on to the then and there. As a minister I have been around death and the dying for what seems my entire life. I have seen death take away my parents, grandparents and many, many relatives. I have sought to comfort family and friends while conducting hundreds of funerals. Yet—this was Judy! Paul asked the rhetorical question, *"O death, where is your sting?"* Sure, theologically I know what he meant. But when Judy died, I knew exactly where that sting was…it was in my heart, my soul, and in the pit of my stomach. It is painful, sharp, and seemingly unrelenting. Does it ever get better?

IT WAS SO FAST

The last week of Judy's life seemed to come out of nowhere. Sure, it has been more than fifteen years since this journey began, but suddenly it's time. One week before Judy's death we saw that her ability to swallow food and fluids was becoming increasingly difficult. That also meant that the administration of her medicines was a challenge. She became more restless, which was exacerbated by her difficulty in taking her meds. Her ability to sit in her recliner, even with pillows stuffed around her, was declining. By Sunday, now entering the last week of life here on earth, those changes were dramatically played out over the course of the day. By Wednesday morning she could no longer sit in her chair and became confined to her bed. Her eyes seemed to try to focus but could not. Although she had long ago lost the ability to talk, her face seemed to speak volumes. Her weary face seemed to say "Please help me" as she tossed and turned in the bed. Just about three weeks earlier we had discovered a busy group of ants had found all the goodies we kept in one of the dresser drawers, and they seemed relentless in their efforts to get their newly found bounty out of the room. Now as the nurses and CNA's scurried in and out of the room, I was reminded of that busy stream of ants working so hard to get those cookies and candy. As mealtime came and went the dietary staff continued to bring her food into the room but try as I might to get a few morsels in her mouth, it was not happening. Liquids were not being swallowed, so I used a little sponge on a stick to swab the inside of Judy's mouth with water. For much of Wednesday she would still bite down on the sponge and the water would be released in her mouth. As the days passed, she lost the ability to clinch her teeth on the sponge which meant that I simply continued to regularly swab lips and mouth with water. Judy's breathing grew shallower and more labored. Her sweet little hands and feet were cold and at times her hands and feet exchanged their natural color for a blueish, purple hue. Sadly, tearfully, I knew the vigil had begun.

I HOPE SHE HEARD ME

Staring at the clock, I for the first time realized that the second hand did not sweep its way around the dial. Instead it seemed to pause at every second and would eventually bump its way along to its next stop. The breathing motion of Judy's chest seemed to be moving in concert with the clock. After each short, shallow breath she seemed to stop breathing. Then there was once again that quick little gasp for air. I passed the time by holding those now frail hands. Hands that once had been so beautiful, and of course, manicured so pristinely. I kissed her furrowed brow and now somewhat sunken

95

cheeks, I talked, and talked, and talked to her...and I prayed and prayed. I have been told my entire life by medical professionals that the ability to hear is the one sense that remains as death nears. With my lips pressed to her ear I repeatedly told her how much I loved her. Wednesday turned into Thursday and Thursday became Friday. She had not opened her eyes since Wednesday. Her breathing was more labored. On Friday evening, as the sun was being swallowed up by the darkness, I knelt by her bed, cradled my arm under her head and once again whispered in her ear. Amid the salty taste of tears, I whispered to Judy that if Jesus and angels showed up in the room and wanted her to go with them it would be okay to go, that she would be safe with them. With Judy's recliner pushed next to her bed I restlessly drifted between the stillness that would for a few moments encase the room, to abruptly rising to check Judy's breathing. Judy had seemed to cherish that recliner. Though long ago she had lost her ability to both walk and talk, that chair had become a means for Judy to express herself. Not only was it a recliner, but a rocker/glider, and it would spin a full 360 degrees. This night all I could think about was all the times I had watched Judy, as she listened to the sixties music which we kept on for her, rocking and spinning around in that chair. Now I sat in that same chair, fearing that her last breath was soon to come, it became impossible to stem the tide of tears.

The RN and the CNA were frequent visitors to Judy's room on that Friday evening. In the very early part of that evening an aide came to check to see if Judy needed to be changed. Her eyes widened and her face was immediately ridden with both astonishment and horror. Jumping to my feet I moved over next to her and the sight was horrific. She and I both were horrified. I was already crying, and I saw tears streaming down her cheeks as well. The RN on duty for that evening had spent many, many years with patients, especially in residential communities, who had some form of dementia. As soon as she saw Judy's back side, she identified it as KTU, Kennedy's Terminal Ulcer, a condition, she explained, she had witnessed with others. It is a rapidly developing sore that appears as the skin begins to breakdown in the final stages of a person's life. The nurse applied ointment and bandages as she tried to address the terror she must have been seeing on my face. Consolation was found only in the fact that Judy's meds by now blocked any possibility of pain. The sun was rapidly setting in my world. Somewhere between 7:30 a.m. and 7:40 a.m. on Saturday morning, October 6, 2018, Judy left that room. I had just kissed her again and sat back into the chair about seven-thirty. The next thing I remember was the sudden realization that I did not hear Judy's labored breathing. The clock said it was seven-forty. Her little hands and face were still warm, but my dear sweet Judy was no longer in the room. Jesus and those angels had come for her and she was safely escorted into that realm that Jesus Himself referred to as paradise. There her memory is restored. She can talk and walk. I believe we all get assignments in heaven, and I have to think that Judy's assignment must somehow include singing and dancing. She is in the company of those she loved long but had since lost. Her parents, my parents, her two sisters…and so many other family and friends who were there to greet her upon her arrival. Her body that had been so infirm, so frail, so weak now rests in the cemetery, but her spirit is soaring, awaiting the resurrection day when body and spirit are united.

CELEBRATION OF LIFE

Judy's memorial service was truly a celebration of the life she had lived and the testimony and witness she left behind. The outpouring of love and care from our church family was beyond amazing. Those who spoke, reminding us of Judy's faith, caused we living to assess and reassess our own lives. The choir, which had been such an important part of Judy's life, sang an uplifting arrangement. The chair in the alto section of the choir which would have been occupied by Judy was draped in a choir robe, and it was adorned with a beautiful white rose and a spotlight marked the spot Judy had faithfully and joyfully filled for so many years. One of Judy's favorite Southern Gospel songs was "I Woke Up This Morning Feeling Fine," and that was sung at the beginning of the service. The great old hymn by Frances Havregal, "Like A River Glorious," was the one that I chose – having been left momentarily behind, it speaks to my heart and my needs.

> Like a river glorious is God's perfect peace,
> Over all victorious, in it's bright increase;
> Perfect, yet it floweth fuller every day
> Perfect, yet it growth deeper all the way.

> Hidden in the hollow of His blessed hand,
> Never foe can follow, never traitor stand;
> Not a surge of worry, not a shade of care,
> Not a blast of hurry touch the spirit there.

> Every joy or trial falleth from above,
> Traced upon our dial by the Son of Love;
> We may trust him fully, all for us to do;
> They who trust Him wholly find Him wholly true.

> (refrain)
> Stayed upon Jehovah, hearts are fully blest
> Finding, as He promised, perfect peace and rest.

THE MINISTRY OF PRESENCE

Three of our ministers spoke at Judy's memorial service, and I was able to make a few remarks as well. It remains unthinkable to me that one would have to experience the kind of long, lingering illness that gripped and took Judy's life without a group of caring and supportive people around them. The last week of Judy's life was made more bearable because of so many who gave me both encouragement and hope. Never underestimate the ministry of presence. Some people avoid the grieving with the excuse, "I don't know what to say." Don't say anything, just be there. And yes, it is okay to cry with the grieving. There is tremendous value in one's presence. Be there when those around you need you the most!

GOODNIGHT BUT NOT GOODBYE

As products of the sixties, Judy and I had a great affinity for the music of that era. In the late sixties the Overtons had a song titled "Goodnight Sweetheart, Goodnight." Some of the lyrics come to mind every time I visit Judy's grave at the cemetery…as in the song, I never want to leave. I linger, I talk to her, I remember what we had together. But, I eventually leave.

Gosh, merely typing those words makes me cry. This is so gut wrenching! I am told, and believe, that time is a healer. God said in the book of Jeremiah that he has plans for each of us, and those plans are not meant to harm us, but to give us a future full of hope. I believe that theologically, but it often escapes me as an emotional reality. Sitting here looking at a photograph of Judy, I am not ready to say goodnight. I know I must get to that place, and I will. I currently find some comfort in the fact that it is goodnight, but not goodbye. For now, let me have my tears. I am just not ready to say goodnight.

10

MAN OF SORROW

Unchanged Melody has always stirred my soul. Judy and I danced to that remarkable song so many times. I can close my eyes even now and feel her head resting on my shoulder as she put her arms around me and held me ever so tightly. Her scent, ever so sweet, wafts through my mind. In each other's arms it was true, time meant nothing. Without a doubt, the most rapturous moment in time, related to that song, came in San Diego, California in 1996. On a hotel rooftop, overlooking the bay, we were dancing no more than ten feet from The Righteous Brothers as they sang *Unchained Melody*. Judy was always beautiful, but that night, in that moonlight, she was breathtaking. I remember never wanting that moment to end. A few weeks following her death in 2018 I made a stop at the funeral home to pick up some memory books and materials that had been prepared for me. The funeral home is adjacent to the cemetery where Judy is buried, so after picking up the books, I decided to drive into the cemetery to visit her gravesite. My mind was absorbed with memories of her, and the life that we had had together, and now we were separated by this graveyard. A fine mist of rain had begun to fall, and just as I pulled to the curb, near the foot of her grave, my thoughts were immediately captured by a little Redbird perched there, and then I realized that *Unchained Melody* was playing on the radio. I froze there...staring at her grave...hearing that song...gripped by the words, that expressed what my aching heart was feeling...even though absent, her presence. She was waiting for me there...soon I would be going home too, and we would once again be together. Amidst tears I drove from the cemetery that day knowing I was returning to an empty house, knowing full well that Judy would not be there to greet me at the door. Yet, I do know that she is waiting for me...in that place where her spirit soars and sings. Another phrase in that song asks what is actually a theological question, will Judy still be mine? The Bible provides (I Corinthians13:12) the only answer I need for that question...who knows, just maybe, our first dance in heaven will be to *Unchained Melody*.

Sorrow is typically defined as grief, a feeling of great sadness. Used as a noun it is defined as distress caused by loss....an occasion of grief. The Bible, in Isaiah 53:3 refers to Jesus as *"a man of sorrows, acquainted with grief."* Within his humanity he certainly experienced grief, such as was visible at the grave of his close friend Lazarus. Gethsemane was a place of great sorrow for Jesus, for it was there that his humanity and deity collided as he prayed on the eve of his crucifixion. He prayed for relief, but the sort of relief that would have silenced the agony of His soul never came. His destiny was the cross and all its horrors. Please, don't think that I am suggesting that my experiences even remotely mirrored His, but my pain, my loss, my grief was real. The seemingly unrelenting waves of sorrow rolled over me and left me gasping for breath. In those moments I could but cling to the hope that somehow I would eventually wash ashore with my sanity intact.

Judy moved to paradise on Saturday, October 6, 2018, just before 7:45 a.m. EST. When I first began this writing project Judy was still living and I fully expected to have it completed long before she died. Following her death, I did not have the desire nor the will to return to the keyboard, and it was March of 2020 before I rekindled my need, yes, my need, to complete the work. I had written *Goodnight Sweetheart, Goodnight* twenty-eight days after her death. Everything in me had suddenly grown numb and cold—there was plenty of emotion, but not the sort that would compel one to sit and write. It was more the sort of emotion that would put you in a sobbing fetal position, hiding in a dark room. This chapter is nothing more than the ramblings and rants that seemed to endlessly stroll through in my soul in the months following Judy's death. Their form was originally nothing more than coarse notes jotted in a little spiral notebook. As I reflect on those notes, I find gaps in time, gaps that I remember as times my mind was too dark to open the window of my soul to allow in any light. My only reason for including any of this is the thought it might help someone else know that it is okay to have those grief filled dark moments, moments often wrought with deep sadness and a notion that it will not get any better anytime soon. But it is also my hope that it provides a window, if only a glimpse, of the reality that we can, all of us, find hope and healing.

Originally, using a pseudonym, C.S. Lewis wrote a little book following the death of his wife Joy, titled *A Grief Observed*. The two married later in life, and she had already been diagnosed with cancer when the two of them met and married. In that regard I cannot relate to Lewis in the expression of anguish and grief found in his book. After all, my Judy was a beautiful, vivacious, and healthy young woman. She was so full of life that it was, in actuality, her trademark. The memories of her expressed in this book bear witness to that fact. Judy was an inseparable part of my life for more than thirty-three years. Lewis and Joy were married but a few years, but it is striking how her death caused him to grieve, even to the extent of examining some of his religious and theological beliefs. Of his grief, Lewis said, "There is a sort of invisible blanket between the world and me." Yes, I can relate to that!

And sometimes I literally pull the blanket over my head in a feeble attempt to keep the world out and Judy in.

Time is a precious commodity, and often in short supply. My time with Judy was not enough. We were both in our mid-thirties, and single, when we met. We married about twenty-eight months after we met, and we were married for thirty-one years, five months and four days. That equates to 11,932 days we were married. It was too short. It ended far too soon. What I wouldn't give for one more day, heck, even one more hour with Judy. I cared for Judy in our home for twelve years. The last three and a half years of her life were spent in a memory care facility, with the last seven months of her life being spent in a long-term care facility. I took great joy in going every day of the week to feed her dinner, and on weekends I fed her both lunch and dinner. I so greatly miss that time. Seeing her, touching her, holding her hand, calling her name, and seeing a little smile cross her face, taking her for rides in a wheelchair, taking her treats and watching with delight as she ate them. Did she ever know that any of those times were taking place? I don't know the answer to that question, but I do know that I knew it, and I miss it. I miss it a lot! I always made sure that I arrived for her evening meal shortly before 5:00 p.m., which meant leaving behind whatever I was doing by 4:30 p.m. There were many times, for a long time after she died, that I kept watch on the clock, thinking about how I need to leave on time to ensure I was there for and with her. It's sort of "funny" in a strange way, how the mind works, isn't it? It will soon be two years since Judy passed away, but there are still afternoons when I glance at a clock and think "it's about time to go." I sure wish that I had had more time with Judy. Where did the time go? Remember, time is the most valuable asset you will ever possess. Don't waste it or just spend it, invest it. Invest that time in those you most love.

Regrets, I have plenty of them. Folks keep telling me that, as regards caring for Judy, during the course of her long battle with Alzheimer's Disease, I have no reason to have regrets. If that is true, why do I often feel the way I do? Could I have talked to her more? Could I have read to her, especially the Bible, more? When she could still talk, did I listen enough? Early on after her diagnosis, did we talk about her fears and did I listen? I have to be careful here. While regrets can be real, and must be dealt with, we cannot forget that our mind can become susceptible to wrong thoughts, misguided thoughts, and even thoughts that our spiritual enemy plants. The Bible reminds us in 2 Corinthians 10:5 to "*take every thought captive.*" We know from science and experience that we have thousands of thoughts every day. Who we are and who we become and what we do is being shaped by those thoughts. With so many thoughts racing through our mind how do we take charge of them? If we take time to read that Bible verse, we discover that God has given us the tools we need to win the battle for our mind. We have the Word of God (Bible) and the Spirit of God (Holy Spirit) as weapons of spiritual warfare to ensure that we do not allow our mind, and thus our life, to be dominated by thoughts and actions that are contrary to God's ways. When the Bible says, "*pray always,*" it means to pray in the moment. When that thought comes, stop, whether literally or figuratively, and pray for God to take it away. Actual regrets can be confessed and forgiveness found. Imagined regrets and guilt can be resolved in a conversation with God.

Prayers are the lifeline of any believer's life. Following Judy's diagnosis, and for years to follow, I prayed for God to heal Judy, as did hundreds of other people. Many of my preacher friends and their congregations prayed for Judy. Missionary friends dotted around the world prayed for Judy. Yet, the disease continued its death march. I then began to pray that God would allow me to live one day longer than Judy. My rationale for that was that I wanted to ensure that all of Judy's needs were met for as long as God allowed her to live. That prayer answer was in the affirmative. I had made every necessary financial and estate plan to ensure her every need would have been met had I died first, but, humanly speaking, I wanted to know that she was never without anything, and I sure wanted her to know that I was there by her side when her last breathe was drawn. My children and grandchildren, all of whom I love immensely, would mourn my passing, but their lives would move on and their needs would be met. Shortly after Judy's death, in a devotional time, I was reading Philippians 1:22-23. As with Paul, my thoughts are, "to depart and be with Christ is far better." Judy is there and I am here. I can only surmise that I am left here because God has something else in mind for me. What's up with that God?

Why? Yes, why? Why, God? Why Judy? Why us? Why now? Why, why, why? Like you, I have learned that that question goes mostly unanswered. Beautiful, bright, talented, loving, caring, kind, generous, loyal…the list seems endless…on and on goes the list that defines Judy. Our best years were still in front of us. We were greatly blessed and our lives seemed to have plenty of wind in the sails. Then came that damning diagnosis. Why? Simple clichés won't suffice. I am not the first to ask, nor will I be the last. Is it wrong to question God? Perhaps. But I know that God understands my kind of loss. I watched my Judy die. He watched His Son die, and furthermore, He made me who I am. But it is just this simple – I am grappling with "why."

"Home is where the heart is," said Pliny the Elder all the way back in early first century. If there is truth in that quote, it helps make sense of why going to my house each night in the months that followed Judy's death left me feeling cold and empty. My house was right where it had been for many years. In fact, while Judy was living in those assisted living facilities, I was living alone in our house. Yet, it was suddenly darker and emptier. I had walked into a dark, empty house for several years, and I did not enjoy it, but I could tolerate it. I could endure the emptiness of the house because the woman I loved was very much alive and I knew I would see her the next day. Her death changed all of that. Now it was empty with no hope of seeing Judy the next morning. I spent countless hours lying in the dark, just staring at the ceiling. There were all those times when, it seemed out of nowhere, a wave of sadness would sweep over me and I would cry what seemed buckets of tears. I can attest that I cried myself to sleep more than a few times. If home is where the heart is, then that house is not home. My heart is elsewhere, my heart is there with Judy. About nine months after Judy died, I put the house on the market to sell it, and I must say that I do not regret moving. After all, my heart was no longer there.

What I wouldn't give just to hear Judy's voice one more time. Alzheimer's had taken away her ability to speak and by the time she died it has been at least four years since she could talk. Occasionally she might say yes or no, but even that was rare. Four years without hearing the voice of someone you love so deeply is torture. While it might not have made a difference, I want to believe that it would have been comforting. And, on many levels, if she and I had been able to have one last conversation it would have been so amazing. Maybe something said would have made us laugh. Perhaps we could have cried together. That opportunity was not afforded me, and frankly, I feel cheated. I try to remember her laugh, the casual banter and even the sometimes stern, well deserved words. But I struggle to remember, and that makes me sad. Goodness, Lord, help me to treasure every word that comes from the lips of those I love.

Special days are, well, special. We all know them and enjoy them… birthdays, Christmas, Easter, the 4th of July…and all those others that make our lives special. Judy loved those special days and she always ensured that those days were going to be celebrated with lots of fun, food, family, and friends. And she always went all out with decorations and all the festive accoutrements needed to guarantee a memorable get together. With Judy Christmas was always over the top at our house. She always wanted the Christmas decorations completed before Thanksgiving. She and a friend, who was a decorator, worked tirelessly while I stayed out of the way and watched. Judy and Mary Jane seemed to get a blast out of getting every little detail just right. That first Christmas without Judy came only 79 days after her death. I was in no mood to celebrate. Mary Jane came and decorated the house, but I didn't really see the point. I cannot help but have visions of Judy scurrying about the house, pulling all those ornaments and trimmings from their yearlong nap. Suddenly the entire house is filled with the sights and sounds of Christmas. A tree towers its way toward the ceiling, covered with hundreds of lights and appointed with all of Judy's treasured ornaments. The house is filled with the scent of cedar and cinnamon wafting through the house. The huge wreath with its hounds-tooth bough adorns the door, and garland weaves it way up the banister. Who am I kidding? That's all in my head. Sure, Mary Jane will come and decorate the house. Yes, my daughters and my grandchildren will all arrive on Christmas Eve. Yes, there will be a dinner party. Yes, we will exchange gifts, and I will somehow cherish every moment. Yet, Judy's chair is empty. It will require great effort on my part to not allow that empty chair to cast a pall over the evening. I cannot go to Rosewood and dress Judy in bright Christmas clothes, and I can't bring her home to spend Christmas Eve with us. My mother always told me not to wish my life away. Sorry Momma. Christmas can't be gone soon enough.

I always saw to it that we made a big deal out of Judy's birthday, even more so as Alzheimer's continued its death march. Judy's first birthday following her death was incredibly painful. I took flowers to her grave and spent more time there than I originally thought I would. I just did not want to leave. The final thing that I did before leaving her gravesite was to sing *"Happy birthday dear Judy...."* I lost my composure and just sat on the grave and wept. To compound the sadness a dear friend died that same week and I officiated his funeral. I am glad that there is no sadness in heaven, and that means Judy was happy on her birthday. For me it was a woeful week. April 22 will always be a day I celebrate Judy in my heart, but I am convinced that eventually those birthdays will be less painful, and that I will celebrate all the joy she brought to my life rather than mourn all that I lost.

The beach is a place where most folks go to relax, just kickback, soak up the sun and enjoy the sights and sounds of the ocean. For Judy, the beach was her version of heaven on earth. We managed to get to the beach several times each year and I can still see her, just seeming to be in her element. Up and down the East and West coast we found beaches that included crowds, and a few that allowed us to be alone. Early in our marriage we were thrilled to find ourselves on the sands of Waikiki and several remote beaches on the Island of Kauai. We lounged on the beaches of the Pacific Highway from San Francisco to Carmel. Who knew that New England had such great beaches? From the Virgin Islands and all across the Caribbean, I still have images of Judy in the sand and the sun. We left our footprints in the beaches of The Gulf of Mexico, all the way from Naples, Florida, then across the Southern states and stretching down to Cancun, Mexico. We even found time for the beach in Israel. I think you get the idea...Judy loved the beach, and if she loved the beach, so did I. During the latter years of her illness there were no beach trips. Since her death, my return to the beach is still a bit strange. My beach time was typically time with Judy, and time with books. I have now been to the beach twice and my books still provide an escape, and goodness, I do enjoy reading. I tend to average about one book per day on beach trips. But now I find myself wandering off within my thoughts, and those thoughts can quickly drift into a world that is melancholy, including a trickle of tears. But, at the same time, that world can quickly become a happy place, after all, it was the place she so loved to be. In that little slice of time I see Judy – lovely as always, luscious lips curled into a broad smile, content with all the world – that moment becomes a happy place for me.

The last several months of Judy's life were almost overwhelming. Every effort we had made for well more than a decade had been rebuffed by the constant grip of the disease. Long hours were spent sitting in Judy's room just watching and waiting…alone. Even before our marriage Judy and I had adopted the idea that together we could accomplish anything and survive everything. There had been times when it seemed that it was the two of us against the world, but we never gave up. Though we could no longer have a conversation about our mantra of never giving up I knew that she and I still had a deep, abiding love that could survive anything. Judy is gone, yet, every time I think about all those times that we prayed and cried, talked and cried, read the Bible and cried, reminisced and cried…it still feels like we could conquer the world. A few of the lyrics from Helen Reddy's song, *You and Me Against the World*, elicits thoughts of Judy, and help to tell our story. Certainly, there were times during the long battle with Alzheimer's that the two of us felt that we alone, fighting the world. Yet, God was always there. In the early years of our marriage, I never imagined that Judy would die before I did. I did everything in advance to ensure that she would be prepared for a time without me. Now she is gone, and I am the one left to carry on. I am left to survive on the memories of her and our life together. As the song says, those memories will get me through.

Solitude. What one does with solitude determines whether it is healthy or hurtful. It is interesting to look in the Bible and see how much time Jesus spent, or at least tried to spend, in solitude. There must have been a reason he often sought solitude. It seems important to distinguish the difference in being alone and being lonely. I have done a lot of both for several years during Judy's long illness. Sometimes we just need to be alone, and I'll come back to that thought. Loneliness was a frequent companion for me, especially as Alzheimer's took more and more of Judy away from me. Oh, I had people around me at the office, at church, and even around me in the facilities when I spent time with Judy. Solitude is being alone by choice and being comfortable with it. Loneliness is far different. Loneliness comes with some pain, and a deep-seated wish or desire to have connection with others. Loneliness can kill you. Science indicates that loneliness has the potential to increase premature death by fifty percent. Cortisol, which in high doses can do damage to the human body, is released when a person is stressed, and medical science knows that periods of loneliness create stress. Even our brain can be damaged by bouts of loneliness. So, even though surrounded by people, how could I have felt lonely? It's simple, having a lot of people around does not equate to a lot of connections. I think that many people, among them widows, widowers, the divorced, caregivers and many others are lonely, and they are lonely because other folks don't know what to do with them, nor do they know how to relate to them. For Judy and me, as her disease worsened, we lost some connections because we were no longer included in certain social settings. I think Judy's "condition" made some people uncomfortable, so it was just easier to not include us in any plans. I can assure you that many recently widowed people feel excluded, having once been a part of a group of other couples, but now those couples find it somewhat uncomfortable, or make a decision for the other person by deciding they don't want to make them uncomfortable. What I am saying here, especially to the church, is to be careful to not exclude, intentionally or unintentionally, those friends who may have had a change in their circumstances or status. We all need connections. Solitude does not always imply loneliness. Jesus often sought alone time, so if it was good for Him, it must serve a purpose in our lives. There are at least six times in the Bible when Jesus pulled aside from others. He sought solitude as a time to pray, to reflect, to recharge. Scripture points out that He used that time to contemplate important decisions, to decompress after long periods of teaching and ministry, and obviously in times of pressure and distress—such as the eve of His death—He turned to time alone with His Father. The great lesson for me, when examining the times of solitude in Jesus' life, is found in Matthew 14:1-13. Jesus had received the news of the tragic death of John the Baptist. John, in terms of ministry, was the forerunner of Jesus, but even more telling is the fact that John was a cousin of Jesus. The brutal end of John's life was startling. The Bible says that when Jesus heard about John's death *"he withdrew from there by boat to a remote place to be alone."* Clearly, He wanted solitude, time to process, time to grieve, time to find comfort through conversation with His heavenly Father. Understanding how Jesus used solitude has helped me move forward. Do I still have times when I feel lonely? Sure! But I have learned that I am never alone.

THOSE WHO MOURN

A ny of us who have been married likely said it. Judy and I certainly did. In fact, as a minister I had said those words many, many times, each time asking the couple to repeat the words for everyone to hear, "...until death do us part." I stood in the chapel of a church on May 2, 1987 and declared my love for Judy, and within the vows I said those very words, "...until death do us part." In the early morning hours of October 6, 2018, I said goodbye to Judy at the same time Jesus said "hello," and my dear Judy was gone. I was left gasping and grasping, knowing what lay ahead for me, but unsure that I was ready to face it. Life without Judy. The Psalmist David, in Psalm 23 wrote about walking through the valley of the shadow of death, and now I found myself walking in those shadows. David somehow survived; I was not certain I would.

I think the most important sermon Jesus ever preached simply declared, *"Repent, for the Kingdom of heaven is at hand."* (Matthew 4:17) Matthew also records a somewhat lengthy sermon of Jesus, known as *The Sermon on the Mount.* Shortly after his message of repentance He was traveling through Galilee and attracting a crowd everywhere he stopped. In order to better see, and to be seen and heard, he ascended a hill, and began another sermon that is recorded in Matthew 5-7. That sermon opens with what we know as the Beatitudes, and second in that list of Beatitudes is the verse that says, "Blessed (happy) are those who mourn, for they shall be comforted. The Message Bible says it this way, *"You're blessed when you feel you've lost what is the most dear to you...."* I can assure you, the day Judy died I had lost what had been most dear to me, but I certainly did not feel blessed.

What I did feel was grief. Sorrow. It is notable that the language of the New Testament, Greek, has no fewer than nine different words for grief, and they all appear in the Bible. The word that Jesus used in Matthew 5:4, mourn, was the word used for grieving death. It is the word used when one who was loved passionately is lost to death. Such grief is accompanied by bitter, uncontrollable tears. It is grief that creates a great whole in our hearts and a throbbing heart pain seems to emanate from that hole...and for some time there can seem little consolation.

WAVES OF GRIEF

As I ponder the entirety of the grieving process, I am firmly convinced that my grief came like the waves of the ocean pounding the beach. My dad passed away suddenly just six days following his sixty-eighth birthday. On a Sunday evening He and I sat by the swimming pool talking about my work, his projects on the house he and mother had recently bought, and of course the kids and grandkids. On Wednesday, during lunch, I received a telephone call from my mother telling me something had happened to Dad. I rushed to their house and arrived just minutes before the emergency vehicles. It was a stroke from which he did not recover. My world was rocked like never before, and the pain and shock was something I had never experienced. At the hospital, when the doctor came out to tell us that he would not recover, I smashed my fist into the wall. Fortunately, my hand was not broken, nor was there a hole in the wall. At the time I could not imagine life without my Dad, and I wondered how long I would have to live without him in my life. In the months that followed I found myself picking up the phone to call him or thinking I would drive over to see he and mother. Perhaps some of the pain was assuaged by turning my attention to Mother and her needs. My fear was how the grief would express itself in her life. My mom drew from the deep well of spiritual reserves, built up by decades of deposits she made based on her relationship with Jesus Christ. She lived twenty-two years longer than my father, and her death came suddenly, but not totally unexpected. The last five of her eighty-six years on this earth were filled with several surgeries, congestive heart failure and significant respiratory issues. I was jolted out of bed at 5:00 a.m.by the telephone call that came from the Hickory Valley Retirement Center, an assisted living residence where Mom had been for just over two years. Given Judy's Alzheimer's, mother was my go-to person about everything. She prayed for me, she encouraged me, she accompanied me on many of the visits to see Judy in the residential memory care facility. Even as her own health was failing and her level of pain often brought tears streaming down her cheeks, she was the Rock of Gibraltar. She died in the wee hours on a Saturday morning—she and I had a dinner date scheduled for that Saturday afternoon, but instead of dinner with me she dined with Dad in heaven that afternoon. I still miss her—her smile, her voice, her words of encouragement, her steadfastness—and I still have moments when I cry. Yet, somehow, because I know how much she longed for heaven, longed to see Daddy, longed to leave behind a body filled with pain…there is sorrow, but not great sadness. Juliet said to Romeo, "parting is such sweet sorrow." Juliet meant that she was not ready to say goodnight, but she found comfort in the fact that she and Romeo would soon see each other again. Although I miss my Mother so very often, I am comforted by the certainly of her faith and mine, that she is with Daddy, and it will not be long now until I see them both.

The grief that I experienced with Judy was anything but sudden. Nor was it the grief that comes when a more aged loved one falls asleep here and wakes up there with Jesus. No, it was more of the world-shaking type of experience. It was the beach being pounded by a category five hurricane type of event. It was sixteen years of excruciating, agonizing grief. Sure, there were respites along the way, but I always knew the next wave would come crashing in over me, flooding me with moments of great despair, never sure of what might happen next. My experience more resembled those video clips I once saw of so-called "Hurricane Hunters" flying directly into a great storm. Those videos show the blunt violent force of the hurricane winds tossing a huge airplane around in the sky, much the way I did as a child when I would toss a toy airplane into the air. Suddenly, the plane would reach the eye of the storm and there would be total calm and no immediate evidence of the storm that was raging all around the calm center of the storm. That best describes my grief experience along Judy's battle with Alzheimer's disease. With Alzheimer's disease the storm never stops raging, and in its path, there is always destruction. An occasional trip into the eye of the storm brings a modicum of peace, but you know the storm itself is still all around.

Within the disciplines of Mental Health, Social Work, Counseling and Psychology there have been many theories of how we humans grieve. One of the first works about grief that I became familiar with was the one posited by Elisabeth Kubler-Ross in a 1969 book titled *Death and Dying*. Prior to her research there had been a few attempts at approaching the subject, but she is typically credited with putting forth the so-called stages of grief. Her work was originally done to describe the process that terminally ill patients go through as they try to come to terms with their own pending reality of dying. The same five stages of grief later came to be applied to those who grieved for the dying. Kubler-Ross stated that the five stages included denial, anger, bargaining, depression, and finally acceptance. No doubt there is merit in the idea of viewing grief in stages, but there are also shortcomings in this concept of stages. Foremost is the notion that one can actually define any of the so-called stages. It seems that so many variables—culture, personality type, family support, community support, church support and so many others—have an impact on how any one person may process grief. I have actually observed clinicians who appear to see the stages as a funnel through which every grieving person must pass, and for grief counseling to be effective the grieving person must pass through every stage, check it off, and move on to the next. Stages of grief is a common thread that runs through the counseling community and it certainly serves as a guide along a path. There can be found literature that proposes anywhere from four stages to twelve stages of grief. Admittedly, by thinking of grief as a process, regardless of the number of stages, it does offer the grieving person the hope that they can navigate through the myriad of emotions and eventually find one's way back to a safe harbor that affords some semblance of security and meaning to life.

CHAOS

Frankly, the thought of stages of grief, which I had been taught in graduate school for counselors, never entered my mind as I walked daily through the reality of Judy's diagnosis. I remembered, and found again, an article written in 1999 by a nursing professor, Linda Rodebaugh. She too uses the term "stages" when describing the grief process, but I suppose I just relate more to the terminology she chose. Her four stages include reeling, feeling, dealing, and healing. Now those are words I can relate to.

From that first day back in October 2003 when Dr. Kodsi told us he was certain that Judy's diagnosis was some form of dementia, I was sent reeling. The doctor had first told us that based on Judy's age and other factors he believed it might be frontal lobe dementia. I remember sitting in front of a computer screen in my office crying. My world was certainly reeling. My mind was racing with all the notions of what that would mean for Judy, what it would mean of us as a couple, what it would mean for our family. I was suddenly thinking about all the plans we had that were not yet realized, and very possibly would never be realized. As I sat there, I suddenly realized that a hand was on my shoulder. As I turned to look, it was one of my business partners and with sadness in her own voice she said, "I am so sorry, and I will pray for you often." As I was soon to know, I was going to need all the prayers Judy and I could get.

Here is why I appreciate Rodebaugh's terminology – those first three terms, reeling, feeling, and dealing became my seemingly constant companion. Judy went through several months of testing and evaluations. Throughout those months of uncertainty there remained hope. But the day the doctor looked us in the eye and said that word, "dementia," the grief began. It is what some clinicians refer to as anticipatory grief. Anticipatory grief begins the day you get a diagnosis that cannot have a good outcome. Reeling and feeling take over. Shock, numbness, disbelief, helplessness, and sadness came rushing in and both of us felt overwhelmed.

My experience and discovery was that the grief never left for those fifteen years. Sure, as mentioned, there were periods of time when the chaos subsided, but it never actually left. Each change in Judy's abilities started the cycle again—reeling, feeling, and dealing. Each change meant Judy had lost a piece of herself…and that I had lost a piece of Judy. Yet, each change meant that I needed to find another way to cope, to deal with, Judy's ever-changing needs. As months became years, the care plan for Judy was in a constant state of flux. I did not recognize it as grief at the time, but I can reflect on every one of those circumstances and understand the reeling and feeling stages that flooded over me at each point of change in Judy's needs. By using the word dealing I am not implying acceptance as much as I mean action. I believe that I was able to numb some of the pain of the grief by dealing with anything and everything that became necessary for Judy's care. Her care, her needs, her safety, her wellbeing was of utmost importance to me. Every change and every crisis required rewriting and reworking the care plan.

On a larger scale dealing with grief implies coping and adapting. I look back on the actions that I took to deal with all of those changes that came at an ever-increasing pace, and those actions helped me grieve the loss and move forward to ensure that Judy's needs could still be met. The loss of traveling and vacationing, the loss of love making, her loss of ability to drive a car, the loss of celebrations, the loss of someone to pour my heart out to, the loss of love, her loss of speech which meant the loss of conversations with her, the loss of her ability to walk, the loss of Judy's ability to eat her meals, the loss of a reciprocal relationship...and on, and on, and on...loss after loss, and I mourned them all. Each succeeding loss brought a new wave of grief. It just seemed like grief compounded, grief on top of grief. Each loss became another time to mourn. When I think of it all I can't help but remember a question posed in the Bible by Gideon when an angel appeared to Gideon and reminded him how God was there for him and how blessed he was. Gideon's response was this question, *"Please sir, if the Lord is with us, why then has all this happened to us? And where then are all His wonderful deeds that our fathers recounted to us....?"* (Judges 6:13) Gideon was facing tough times, and I assure you he is not the only fellow to ask that question.

I did discover that healing comes intermingled with the reeling, feeling, and dealing. Perhaps that is why I don't often use the terminology applicable to the stages of grief. That notion seems to imply that if I work the steps and check the box, all in some orderly fashion, then in a neatly packaged box I will arrive at that place where life is good again. Be certain, I believe we can arrive at that "good" place. But it can be a circuitous route, full of zigs and zags, starts and stops, good days and bad days. It can be a sprint, or it can be a marathon. In retrospect, healing, along with all the feelings, the reeling and even the dealing, that comes with grieving are interwoven in such a way that most hearts can be mended to the degree that one can look forward, even if we continue to glimpse back. Healing does not mean that our loss is forgotten. Healing does mean that we can learn to live with the loss. Healing leads us toward hope.

FAITH-HOPE-LOVE

The Bible fits these three words together several times. Found in Romans 5:1-5 is a marvelous confession of faith that declares the place of faith, hope, and love in our salvation. In 1 Thessalonians 1:3 the Apostle Paul offers a commendation to a group of believers who have repeatedly demonstrated a life built on faith, hope and love. Paul makes a similar comment to yet another group of believers in Colossians 1:4-5. In perhaps the best-known scripture about these three virtues Paul said, *"So now faith, hope, and love abide, these three: but the greatest of these is love."* (1 Corinthians 13:13) Recovery and mending for broken hearts rests in these three powerful elements. Faith looks to the past, that is all that God did for me in Christ Jesus, including manifesting the greatest act and gift of love ever known when at the cross Jesus died as my substitute. Hope is about the future. In Romans 8:25 Paul said, *"...we hope for what we do not see...."* Hope claims the future and does so with great confidence. Love is about today and the fact that God loves me in the here and now. Some read 1 Corinthians 13:13 with a bit of sentimental sloppiness. Faith declares that God did something wonderful for me, hope says he has a future for me, and love says that he shows up every day for me. It is faith, hope and love that heals and fills us with hope.

The Old Testament contains this marvelous verse, *"But this I call to mind, and therefore I have hope."* (Lamentations 3:21)

Lamentations is a book about tears. The Bible does not try to shelter us from grief and the tears that come with that grief. In the gospel of John is the story of a funeral attended by Jesus. Upon seeing the weeping of the sister of the deceased, John 11:33 states, *"When Jesus saw her (Mary) weeping...he was deeply moved and his spirit greatly troubled."* At the graveside John 11:35 records just these two words, *"Jesus wept."* The tears that accompany our grief are welcomed by God. Following Judy's death, I spent countless hours in a dark room, staring at the ceiling, crying, even wailing before God. Washington Irving said, *"There is sacredness in tears. They are not the mark of weakness, but of power. They speak more eloquently than ten thousand tongues. They are the messengers of overwhelming grief, of deep contrition, and of unspeakable love."*

It seems that God gave us tears for our benefit. Crying activates the parasympathetic nervous system (PNS). The PNS helps our body rest and actually improves digestion. Tears also dull pain. Crying releases oxytocin and endogenous opioids, known as endorphins.

Released into our body, they can lead to a numb-like state. Remarkably, those same tears have the ability to improve our mood. Crying tends to cause us to take in quick breaths of cool air, and that air helps regulate the brain and to lower the temperature of the brain, and a cool brain is happier than a warm brain. So, even though our grief can seem relentless and cause us to feel hopeless, there is a way through the daunting course of grief.

These three simple statements have helped me replenish the hope that had been diminished by the heaviness of grieving.

First, hope returns when we renew our faith. Jeremiah, our writer in Lamentations, points us to the fact that our hope is renewed, not by doing, but by waiting. In Lam. 3:25 he said, *"The Lord is good to those who wait for him, to the soul who seeks him."* For a person with my type A personality, waiting is not exactly an easy task. Now, give me a task, give me an assignment, and I am on it. Better yet, give me a deadline for the task and get out of my way. But wait? Well, that's not so easy. This may sound strange, but I have to be deliberate, intentional in putting myself in a waiting mode. Even more strange...I had to develop a plan for waiting (on God). So here we go:

- Scripture—here I don't mean hard core Bible study— Psalms 46:10 says, *"Be still and know that I am God."* I have to still myself with devotional time, and I have to be careful that it does not turn into sermon preparation. This is waiting, not working.
- Silence is golden—create alone time—I like to be busy; I love being around people. When I write lesson plans and prepare sermons, I play music in the background. And I don't mean church music...I mean the "golden oldies." So, I have to be able to still myself and silence myself.
- Singing—the worship music of today is good; it is just that I'm a hymn sort of guy. I get swept away by the splendor of the music and its message. The point here is that waiting needs to include worship time.

- Surrender—the hymn says, *All to Jesus I surrender, all to Him I freely give; I will ever love and trust Him, In His presence daily live. All to Jesus I surrender, Lord I give myself to thee; Fill me with Thy love and power, Let Thy blessing fall on me.*
- Sort—capture your thoughts during your time of waiting. Write them down and then sort through them. Some will be good thoughts and those are the keepers. Toss the others in the trash and forget them.

Isaiah 40:31 says, *"They who wait for the Lord shall renew their strength; they shall mount up with wings like eagles; they shall run and not be weary; they shall walk and not faint."* Now that's hope. Jesus added to that thought when he said, *"Come to me all who are weary, and I will give you rest."* (Matthew 11:28) Grief is wearisome, but hope is on the horizon as we wait and trust God.

Next, hope returns when we respond to Scripture. In Lamentations 3:40 are found these instructions, *"Let us test and examine our ways, and return to the Lord."* Exams and tests are something we can all relate to based on both our educational and life experiences. This test, like those from our school days, comes with a textbook. The textbook for this test is the Bible, and the challenge from the verse is that we truly seek to align ourselves with God's word. As I read that third chapter of Lamentations, it struck me that the scripture is providing us with a pathway to hope. The pathway includes:

- Remember—verse 21 says, *"Call to mind…."* For me that leads me in two directions. The first is that I can, and do, remember all the joy and all the fun that Judy and I enjoyed. I even find a measure of comfort in remembering the privilege it was to care for Judy as the disease took more and more of her away from me. When we suffer great losses we have a choice to make. We can choose to dwell on all that we lost, all the grief that we experienced along the way or, we can choose to spend more time thinking about all the shared joy God brought into our lives by giving us the time we had with that loved one we have lost. Sure, I still miss Judy. Sure, tears still come when special remembrances come to mind. Sure, I wish we had been among those couples that get the gift of living to a "ripe old age" together. Yet, even in the throes of what could turn to despair I make a deliberate choice to remember all the good, all the joy, all the shared experiences that she and I had for so many wonderful years. Then, most of all, I take time each day to remember the goodness of God.

- Seek him—verse 25 reminds us to wait on the Lord, but it also goes on to say, *"the Lord is good…to the soul that seeks him."* Grief can numb us to spiritual things if we are not careful. I learned long ago that God can handle not only my praise, but my complaints as well. While it is true that God is always present, it is also true that times come into our lives when we need to seek His presence. The Psalmist said, *"seek the Lord…seek His presence continually."* (Psalm 105:4)

- Pray—Lamentations 3:55-57 says, *"I called on your name, O Lord, from the depths of the pit; you heard my plea. Do not close your ear to my cry."* When the disciples of Jesus asked Him to teach them to pray, He responded with a model prayer, that we often refer to as "The Lord's Prayer." Have you ever noticed how much time Jesus spent in prayer, and most often His prayers focused on others rather than Himself. In the seventeenth chapter of John's gospel is found what is truly the Lord's prayer. It is a lengthy intercessory prayer in which He appeals to the Father on behalf of His followers, both those then as well as all of us who followed in the ensuing centuries. The Methodist preacher, E.M. Bounds, said, *"God shapes the world by prayer. Prayers are deathless. The lips that utter them may be closed in death, the heart that felt them may have ceased to beat, but the prayers live on before God, and God's heart is set on them and prayers outlive the lives of those who uttered them; they outlive a generation, outlive an age, outlive a world."* I remember from the early years of my ministry as a pastor I had a plate attached on the front of my car that proclaimed, "Prayer Changes Things."

Indeed, prayer does change things, but in the course of time I learned that what changed the most because of my prayers was me. Prayer changed my outlook. Prayer changed my thoughts. Prayer changed my evaluation of my circumstances. Prayer changed my approach to problems and trouble. Prayer changed my reaction to circumstances. In the darkness of my grief, prayer changed me.

- Don't allow fear to control you—Lamentations 3: 57 reminds us of God's provision when it says, *"You (God) came near to when I called on you; you said, 'Do not fear!'"* Fear can be debilitating. It is so easy, and is our human inclination, to allow fear to capture our thinking when we are faced with the great uncertainly that floods our spirit when news comes about a difficult diagnosis, or a damaging set of circumstances, or the death of a loved one. We might even say that fear is natural, however, we do not have to allow that fear to take up residence on our life. The Bible holds many words of encouragement and hope in how to gain a supernatural (rather than natural) approach to fear. From Joshua 1:9 comes this encouragement, *"...be strong and courageous. Do not be terrified; do not be discouraged, for the Lord your God will be with you wherever you go."* 2 Timothy 1:17 records, *"...God did not give us a spirit of fear, but a spirit of power..."* Just remember, all of us have fears at various times in our life. It happens! But we do not have to get stuck in that place of fear. We must learn to do what King David did in moments of mounting fear, *"When I am afraid, I put my trust in you. God, I have put my trust in you....in God I trust...I shall not be afraid."* (Psalm 56:3-4) When we allow fear to dominate our thoughts, we become powerless, which then can lead to a sense of hopelessness. Scripture admonishes us to take charge of our lives.

- Take back your life—David, in Psalms 34: 4,6, 17 said, *"I sought the Lord, and He answered me and delivered me from my fear...this poor man cried, and the Lord heard him and saved him from his troubles...when the righteous cry for help, the Lord hears and delivers them out of all their troubles."*

Finally, hope returns when we replace sorrow with joy. Jeremiah the prophet said, *"For the Lord will not cast me off forever, but though he causes grief, He will have compassion according to the abundance of his steadfast love..."* (Lamentations 3:31-32) What can rob us of our joy? Within the context of this book we are talking about the grief that comes from losing someone we have loved deeply and completely. But we know that the loss of joy can also come from many other human experiences, which can include envy, jealousy, anger, bitterness, doubt, lack of faith, sin, unforgiveness, greed and selfishness. It was David who, in Psalm 51:12, cried out to God, *"Restore to me the joy... and uphold me with a willing spirit."*

Perhaps there is no greater illustration of the restoration of hope and joy than what is brought to mind in a somewhat obscure verse in the Bible. In Hosea 2:15 is found this message, *"And there I will give her her vineyards and make the Valley of Achor a door of hope."* Isn't that what we are looking for when waves of grief come crashing in and seem to swallow us in hopelessness? A way out, an end to the endless crying, an end to all the doubts and fears and worries, an end to the dread that seems to arrive afresh every morning. Aren't we looking for a door of hope? The first major victory won by Israel as they finally entered the land that God had long, long ago promised to them was the fall of the city of Jericho. It was a highly fortified city with an army that was both sizable and highly skilled. The Israelites had no such army and appeared to be over matched, and as we read the story in the book of Joshua, God used some unusual methods to allow the city of Jericho to fall to the Israelites. By the time they arrived at the next obstacle, a town named Ai, they were still living in the glow of the last victory and underestimated their next opponent, and worse than that, they ignored God's game plan that He had provided for them. The outcome was an embarrassing disaster. It was the equivalent of the Tennessee Titans losing to Tennessee Tech University. Things like that are not supposed to happen. Yet here it is recorded in the Bible and we still hear about it and read about it more than 3,000 years after it happened. Here is the point—that little city of Ai was located in the Valley of Achor. The Valley of Achor became associated with great personal losses. Some of the Israelites lost their lives, the others were chased away, and it was such a public humiliation that Joshua tore his clothes (a sign of grief) and fell on the ground. Of the Israelites it was said, *"And the hearts of the people melted and became as water."* (Joshua 7:5) I grew up hearing an old expression, "weak as water." Even as a kid I knew that meant a lack of will, a lack of heart, a lack of resolve or strength, faint hearted. Grief can make us "weak as water." Grief causes our hearts to melt. So, it was in this Valley of Achor that pain and sorrow, defeat, and death, found its way into the lives of the Israelites. Why then does Hosea 2:15, many years later, refer to this same Valley of Achor as a *"door of hope?"* Why? Because that is the way God works. When we align ourselves with the Word of God, and we pray and seek God, and we cast out fear, then wonderful hope and peace comes flooding in to heal our hearts, bind up our wounds and replace sorrow with joy.

Horatio Spafford, a well to do lawyer in Chicago, wrote the words to the great hymn *It Is Well With My Soul.* The opening verse contains these lyrics…

> When peace like a river attendeth my way,
> When sorrows like sea billows roll;
> Whatever my lot, thou hast taught me to say,
> It is well with my soul.

He penned those words following a great family tragedy. His son had died at an early age, and then his remaining four daughters, while traveling to England, perished at sea. How does one rise above such tragedy? Spafford, who was an elder in his church, and spoke freely of his faith in Christ, drew upon the spiritual reserves that resided in his own soul. There is no other explanation, given so much loss and so much grief, that could lead him to the conclusion that "it is well with my soul."

May all of us, who may be reeling in grief, feeling left out and left behind, bring into all our attempts to deal with our losses, open hearts to allow God to be our healer. May we find, in the words of the Apostle Paul the kind of peace that passes all human understanding. May we all claim as our own, the promise of God, *"I will restore your health and heal your wounds, declares the Lord..."* (Jeremiah 30:17)

PARADISE FOUND

In 1667 John Milton, considered one of the great English poets, published a set of writings with the title, "Paradise Lost." He had begun the work in 1658, and by this point in his life Milton was blind, so therefore he dictated, and another person wrote for him. "Paradise Lost" was the tale of Eden and how Adam and Eve, under the influence of Satan, disobeyed God and they were then directly expelled from the Garden of Eden. Speaking to a dying thief on an adjoining cross, Jesus, in response to a statement from the thief said, *"Today you will be with me in paradise."* Both the thief and Jesus were nearing death and Jesus is clearly not talking about paradise lost. Rather, Jesus makes a promise to the dying man, that they would both soon be found in paradise. Yes, paradise was lost because of the actions of Adam and Eve, but paradise is found because of the action of Jesus.

My mother, Iva Glass Johnston, died on July 15, 2017. Judy passed away on October 6, 2018. I certainly consider myself a person of faith. For more than half a century I have been preaching and teaching the Bible. I have stood with families at the bedside of their dying loved ones. I have stood at the head of hundreds of graves as families laid loved ones to rest. I believe I have a good theological understanding of the biblical teachings regarding death and the afterlife. At the same time, I readily confess, that like so many others I have known, upon the loss of Mom and my wife I sought fresh assurances from scripture concerning what happens when a Christian dies. So, as I often do when pressed by some thought or question, I read and studied the Bible looking for comfort, reassurance, and fresh revelation, along with inspiration. Most often when I do that it becomes a Bible study series that I then share with the Bible class I have been teaching for more than thirty years. My focus for that study was heaven. I wanted to ensure that I had the most comprehensive understanding of paradise and heaven that I could have. Whatever heaven is, or will be, I now had a huge investment there in that place. Both of my parents and Judy have moved on to there. Where are they now? What are they doing? Does Judy spend time with my parents? Who else are they visiting with each day? Gosh, is there even such a thing as day and night? So many questions, so much I wish I could know. What can be known is only that which we can obtain from the Bible.

GLIMPSES OF GLORY

A giant peach welcomes travelers along Interstate 65 to Clanton, Alabama. Yes, a peach. Clanton, the geographical center of the State of Alabama, has for its city water tank a giant peach. You see, Clanton is peach country. One can hardly travel through Clanton without a stop at one of numerous roadside vendors selling peaches. And wow, the homemade peach ice cream at the intersection of I-65 and Highway 31 is out of this world.

In the late seventies, in Clanton, I had one of the most productive pastorates I ever had the privilege of serving. I was twenty- six years of age when I moved to Clanton to pastor Friendship Baptist Church. It wasn't long before the church walls were bursting at the seams. We had multiple buses and a productive bus ministry, families were joining, and we were blessed to see many people make professions of faith. We once had an evangelistic meeting in which seventy-two people professed Christ. There was one Sunday evening in which I was privileged to baptize thirty-seven people who had come to faith in Christ. Our youth ministry was teeming with excitement and the children's ministry had outgrown it space. We had an outstanding ministry for the deaf. And then there was "Glimpses of Glory." God gave me a vision for a broadcast ministry for the church and our deacons were immediately onboard with the idea and launched "Glimpses of Glory." I chose that for the name of our broadcast based on two passages from the Bible that involved people who were allowed, and blessed, to catch glimpses of glory.

First, in Matthew 17: 1-8, Peter, James, and John, along with Jesus Christ, found themselves atop a mountain. The Bible does not identify the mountain by name, but that has not prevented people from speculating as to its location. While we may not know the name of the place, we do know what happened atop that mountain. Those disciples witnessed something remarkable and miraculous, an event that Christians refer to as the Transfiguration. Standing right before them those disciples saw Jesus as they had never seen him before. His entire appearance and countenance were changed. In the Bible we learn that Jesus willingly stepped aside from His place in heaven in order to take on the form of a man, and to even die as a man, and in dying made redemption possible whereby lost sinners can be saved. On that mountain, at that precise moment, those three disciples briefly saw what no other person had ever seen. For a brief moment they caught a glimpse of His glory.

In 2 Corinthians 12: 1-10 Paul writes about a very unusual experience. He states that he was caught up into the third heaven, and then he makes a reference to paradise. There are two other references to paradise in the New Testament. We have already alluded to the Luke passage in which Jesus told the dying thief that he would be joining him in paradise. John writes in Revelation 2:7 about a place that is the paradise of God. Those things seen by Paul when he made a visit to paradise left him speechless. He was taken

131

to heaven and then back to earth. Without a doubt Paul caught a glimpse of glory. There is a wonderful lesson for us to take from this event. We appear able to determine that for some reason Paul did not reveal this trip to heaven with anyone. In an effort to establish a timeline we can place this event in about 43 A.D., or that period of time captured by Luke in Acts chapters nine, ten and eleven. It was during that time period that Paul experienced some of his most horrendous days. In his first letter to the Corinthians he alludes to the long list of haunting, horrible, and harrowing experiences, several of which almost cost him his life. Could it be that God showed him heaven in order to prepare him for the trials that were to come into is life, and which would eventually cost him his life? Could it be that Paul's fast and firm faith was bolstered by the reality of heaven and all that awaited him there? Yes, I absolutely think so, in much the same way all of us are encouraged and comforted by what we know from the Bible about heaven. Like Paul we can find spiritual stamina for the journey as we continually catch glimpses of glory.

THE PROMISE OF PARADISE

Two dying men once had a very brief conversation regarding the matter of the afterlife. Both had been sentenced to death, one of them for living a life of crime, the other for being the Son of God. The Bible records the brief conversation. The dying criminal, in rebuking the taunts of a third dying man, said of Jesus, the Son of God, *"And we indeed justly, for we are receiving the just rewards of our deeds; but this man has done nothing wrong. And he said 'Jesus, remember me when you come into your kingdom.' And he said to him, 'Truly I say unto you, today you will be with me in paradise."* (Luke 23: 41-42) There it is, a promise, from the Son of God Himself. Paradise!

It is to this place called paradise that our dear loved ones who have died and moved on into eternity go. Paradise is that third heaven that Paul was talking about in his letter to the Corinthians. It is the place that is beyond the reach and scope of our knowledge. It is outside the atmosphere that we understand, it is beyond what we call outer space. It is the third heaven; it is paradise.

It is also this promise of paradise that Jesus used to comfort his disciples when he was explaining to them that his time on earth was growing short, and that he would, for a time, be leaving them behind. John 14:1-6 captures the essence of what Jesus taught those disciples regarding paradise. Preachers have long used this passage of Scripture as a message of hope and comfort at funerals, and why not? Jesus meant it as such for his followers.

There is much hope and encouragement found in this passage. First and foremost are the powerful words of Jesus, words that speak of the *PEACE OF CHRIST, "Let not your hearts be troubled, Believe in God, also believe in me."* Certainly, *troubled hearts* find their way into all of our experiences from time to time. On this particular day, as I write, we are still sitting in the wake of a global pandemic from the coronavirus. People I personally know have died from the disease. I have officiated funerals for those who died from the disease. It seems the newscasters can talk about nothing else. It is ever-present. Troubled hearts come our way when our children are hurting. Troubled hearts come when we get bad news from a doctor. Troubled hearts come when loved ones die. In the months following Judy's death I cried because I missed her. I cried because I was alone. I cried because the woman I loved was gone and I knew that in this life I would never hold her hand or kiss her cheek again. I cried at the mere mention of her name. I cried on every visit to the cemetery. I truly had a broken, troubled heart. However, one should not dismiss the words of Jesus that direct us to our need to have a *trusting heart.* The words of Jesus are remarkable. He is telling us that in our most troubling circumstances that we can place our full confidence in God and His abilities, and Jesus goes on to inform us that He (Jesus) is the one who will bring to us the support, provision, protection and comfort of God. Jesus offered these words to the disciple in the darkest of times. He was soon to be betrayed, put through a sham of a trial, beaten almost to death, and then brutally nailed to a cross. Yet here Jesus is thinking about what the disciples are about to face. Those men had given up everything to follow Him, and now they would be left alone. Beyond the grief would come chaos, confusion, and a rush to hide themselves from all that was happening. The pain and confusion, and even the chaos that came after Judy's death brought thoughts of hiding from it all. So many people do hide their feelings, all while trying to maintain composure for the benefit of others. When trouble comes to us, we have choices. Some choose to hide behind a façade of composure, others choose to hide behind unhealthy habits, and others choose to immerse themselves in grief with little to no hope of recovery. Jesus Christ offers us an alternative. He offers us hope and courage that can enable us to rise from the ashes. Jesus says, *"...don't be troubled or afraid."* It is Jesus Christ who sits between God and us, and it is He who provides us with an open passage to communicate with God. Jesus Himself demonstrated what it was like to have a troubled heart, for in the very moment he said these words, He stood at the threshold of Gethsemane where his troubled heart would bring blood droplets from his body. So, He who knew what a troubled heart felt like, said, trust me and believe me when I tell you I will take care of that for you. So, in this space of time we refer to as the "here-and-now" while we await the "here-after," we must learn to rest in the peace of Christ, for He said, *"I am leaving you with a gift – peace of mind and heart. And the peace I give is a gift the world cannot give. So don't be troubled or afraid." (John 14:27 NLT)*

As we read John 14 our thoughts are also directed to the *PREPARATION OF CHRIST.* To the disciples he offered a word of *confirmation* when he states, *"In my Father's house are many rooms. If it were not so, would I have told you that I go to prepare a place for you?"* Jesus confirms ample room is available and awaits us in the Father's house. Jesus also makes a comforting statement relative to the fact that His followers already have a *reservation* in paradise. Those earlier disciples, and all believers since, are not left to wonder if they will make it to heaven. Jesus affirms that our reservation is being held for us until we get there. It is a reservation guaranteed by an advance deposit. In Ephesians 1:13-14 Paul states, *"...you...were sealed with the promised Holy Spirit, who is the guarantee of our inheritance until we acquire possession of it..."* Our guaranteed reservation ensures that our room is ready and waiting when we arrive. In fact, Jesus also speaks about our eventual *occupation* by saying, *"...I will come again and take you to myself, that where I am you may be also."* One might ask how we will get there? Will we travel alone? Will we be afraid? Those questions made me think of a billboard I once saw in my city. There was a group photo of real estate agents on the billboard and the billboard proclaimed them to be the "relocation experts." The Bible certainly seems to strongly suggest that God too has a collection of relocation experts, and they are called angels. We are not left to make the journey from this life into the next on our own; we will be accompanied by angel guides. Jesus told a story (Luke 16) about two men who had died. One, who had not lived a godly life found himself in the torments of hell, while the second man (Lazarus) who was a poor sick man, but obviously a lover of God, had been escorted by angels into paradise (God's presence). I believe that early on that Saturday morning on which Judy's spirit departed from her frail body, angels had been dispatched to see her safely into paradise. Not for a moment did she have to be fearful or concerned about the route. She had a heavenly escort to show her to her new room. Her old room was filled with sickness, tears, and death. Her new room was glorious beyond imagination! That wonderful song by MercyMe, *"I Can Only Imagine,"* says it best. I read the Bible and try to imagine what it must be like, that is to be standing in His presence, the entire scene filled with His splendor and glory. Dancing, singing, speaking? I am not sure, but I do know that I will fall to my knees in His holy presence.

Like many who have seen loved ones move on to paradise, I often contemplate what that must be like for Judy. I know that she is free from any disease that took over her body. From the Bible I can ascertain that she is still getting acquainted with folks like Abraham, David, and Isaiah. Perhaps she and Eve have had conversations, Eve discussing Adam and Judy perhaps mentioning Alan. Judy is perfectly at home with all the worship and all the singing.

Sometimes at our church I mumble a bit about the volume of the sound system during the worship service. It often seems that the sound crew only knows three settings...loud, louder, and loudest. I suspect that no one in heaven complains about the volume, or the length of the worship service. Goodness, at the great times Judy and I had sitting in Bryant Denny Stadium in Tuscaloosa cheering (screaming) for the Crimson Tide. The stadium crew measures the decibels of the crowd noise, posts it on the video screens, and then prompts the crowd inside the stadium to get even louder. One CBS crew member said that while working an Alabama versus Florida game in Tuscaloosa that the noise was so loud that he could not hear the production director through his noise cancelling headphones. Heaven will be louder and grander than anything we have imagined and the sound of our worship in heaven will resound throughout the heavens. John's Revelation repeatedly describes the songs and sounds of heaven. Yes, I know Judy is singing and worshipping even now. But paradise, while filled with awesome worship, is more than an eternal worship service. When Judy is not worshipping or resting, she is perfectly fulfilled with the work assigned to her, and she is perfectly delighted with the time she spends with others, for she and all others live there in a perfect relationship. There is no envy, no jealousy, just perfect relationships. Most important of all, Judy is Judy! She is not some nebulous, disembodied spirit. She is Judy. Only now—she is Judy perfected. She now has "heavenly DNA" that knows no wrong, no sin, and is perfected in character, and in knowledge, because of her relationship with Jesus Christ. When I arrive in paradise, I will know Judy as Judy. No, we will not have a marriage relationship, for Jesus stated that paradise would not include such relationships. But we will know each other, and she and I will know and live among all the others who are residents of paradise.

We must not neglect the fact that there is a singular route to paradise. That only way is the *PATHWAY OF CHRIST*. In response to the questions presented by Thomas, Jesus made this reply, "*I am the way, and the truth, and the life; no one comes to the Father except through me.*" Yes, it is true. Jesus Christ, based on our confession of faith in him and our renouncing of sin and self, is the only way. It is our declaration that He alone is Lord that ensures that our name is in the reservation book and that it can never be erased. It is that faith in Him that ensures a wonderful welcome party when we arrive in paradise.

HEAVEN ON EARTH

We often say, or hear others say, that something, or some place, offers a little bit of "heaven on earth." Why, I said that myself in regard to my life with Judy prior to her Alzheimer's diagnosis. When she came into my life it was as though the favor of heaven rested on my head and the road came up to meet my feet. Yes, it was heaven on earth. But, while I considered my time with Judy to be divine, I mean something much more regarding heaven on earth. Heaven on earth is not some ethereal experience in the here and now. Rather, it is a future reality. As we have discussed, Christians die and pass on from this earth to reside in the presence of Jesus Christ in paradise, which is in fact described in the Bible as the third heaven. Let us not forget there is more in store. There is yet to come a fourth heaven, a heaven defined and described by the Bible as heaven on earth. In Revelation 21:1-2 the Apostle John shared a vision, a revelation that God gave to him, *"Then I saw a new heaven and a new earth, for the first heaven and first earth had passed away, and the sea was no more. And I saw the holy city, new Jerusalem, coming down out of heaven from God...."* In Revelation 21:5 John recorded the words of the One he saw seated on the throne, *"...behold I am making all things new."*

In the Bible, in Peter's second letter, we can find some information regarding the old earth and how God intends for all that is old to pass away in order that all things can be made new. While Peter does briefly mention that the earth is going to melt away, the Bible does not give us any significant details as to how God plans to remove or destroy earth as we know it, only that He will. Our ultimate future, beyond paradise, is on an earth that is fully recreated by God. Every trace of all that we know to be wrong, harmful, and hurtful will be gone. As Isaiah the prophet said, God will create a new heaven and a new earth and no remnant of the old will remain, in fact, no recollection of it will come to our memory. Wow, heaven on earth, what a glorious day that will be when we see Jesus! Seeing Him will overshadow all of what we presently experience, and fade in the light of His unending glory.

PRECIOUS MEMORIES

Across more than fifty years of ministry, I have officiated hundreds of funerals. I always found the funeral music selections to be interesting. When my Mother died, we selected *It Is Well With My Soul* as one of the selections. That seemed so appropriate for my Mother. When Judy died, we selected several songs, ranging from hymns to Southern gospel. The hymn selection was *Like A River Glorious* that speaks to the perfect, abiding peace found in that place God hides us in in times of trouble. Across the years, especially those early years serving in rural churches, there were a few songs that never had much appeal to me. One of those was a song by the title *Precious Memories*. I suppose it was the slow, mournful cadence with which it was typically sung that I never found very uplifting. However, when it comes to Judy, there are so many precious memories.

These are the memories and reflections of both family and friends, all of whom knew Judy so well, and all of whom retain many precious memories of Judy:

FAMILY

Judy was such a wonderful gift to our family. She quickly became the sister that I never had. And, oh my, our mother and daddy fell in love with Judy and absolutely cherished and adored her—and they were so thankful that God brought Judy into Alan's life. The entire Johnston family was in love with Judy. Make no mistake, Judy loved my brother, and she was quick to tell anyone just how much she did love him. Her love wasn't only evident in her words, but in her actions as well.

Judy had many gifts, and one of those was to make people feel special. I was always a somewhat shy person, and Judy was the opposite. She would light up a room with her sweet smile, loving charm and had an innate ability to make anyone laugh. Judy could do what few others could do—make our daddy laugh.

Judy's smile and striking beauty was amazing. I have never met anyone who loved to sing and dance as much as Judy. I shared her love of music and dancing and one of my favorite memories is that on our frequent trips to the beach the two of us would spend hours, in a hotel room or a condo at the beach, dancing and dancing. Even after her memory had begun to falter, she could still sing and dance.

Judy shared a wonderful quality with our mother—kind heartedness and unselfishness. She would always be willing to stop whatever she was doing and sit and listen to you. I have learned that is a rare gift, and it was a gift that came naturally to Judy. Our entire family loved Judy and we are richer for having her in our family. I loved Judy, and I miss her in our family.

Donna Johnston Dunagan

Northport, AL

Judy joined our family when I was a young teenager, and sadly, it was at a point in time when I hated most everyone, including myself. She tried to show love and kindness, but I was not at a place in my life where I could, nor knew how, to accept it. We clashed on so many things, so many times, for so many reasons – yet, she was always patient, kind and loving in her responses. My own life outlook began to shift and much of my personal bitterness had begun to dissipate, and there was Judy, who remained unchanged through it all. Today I can look back and recall so many wonderful memories because Judy was in my life. She was always, and I mean always, constant, persistent, gracious, generous and thoughtful. Judy would have been willing to, as they say, "give you the shirt off her back." She was a marvelous cook, and anytime we were going to be in Judy and Dad's home for a meal, she ensured the food was prepared to our liking.

One striking memory is that of Judy's excitement at Christmas time. She shopped all year long for all of us. She would hide the presents in the attic, closets and any other crevices she could find. She just kept on shopping. Her motto was "out of sight, out of mind...so shop, shop shop!" By Christmas Eve we would have so many presents under the tree and she would be upstairs finding and wrapping even more gifts. Christmas at Dad and Judy's was always terrific—lots of laughs, lots of great food, and of course, lots of great presents. As already said, Judy was so kind, loving and generous.

Joy Johnston Clemons

Chattanooga, TN

I was nine years old when Dad met Judy. He had dated some, but never anyone for any long period of time. Frankly, I was less than excited about any of them, and was always relieved when Dad moved on. But then along came Judy. Even as young as I was, I recognized that she was the "one." He was just different around her, and when he talked about her it was even more obvious. They eventually dated for more than a couple of years and were then married.

Eventually they were married – and I was not a happy camper! I made it my goal to "torture" her and to do anything I could to make life difficult for her. I made certain she knew that she was not my mother and that I wanted nothing to do with her. I am not sure how she tolerated my behavior, and Dad was always trying to encourage me and coach me to be more tolerant and more kind. It took a couple of years, but I finally gave up the mean, hateful attitude toward Judy. Suddenly the realization hit me in the face – not only was she so wonderful to and for my Dad – but she actually loved my sister and me and was working hard to be a blessing to us. And, she was!

I remember those early years on Concord Road. Dad had a swimming pool installed, and I can still see Judy in that pool, wearing a ski belt Dad had bought her, practicing, to improve her swimming skills. Later at the house in Shadow Ridge there was also a swimming pool and there we spent so many hours in that pool with Judy. Judy and I spent many hours in the sun, around and in that pool. It obviously became one of my favorite things to do. I do not remember a time when Judy did ensure all of our favorite foods were hand. As I think back, I now remember how when it was time to wake up in the morning, she would show up with a Mountain Dew in her hand, and I could always talk her into a quick "back scratch." That would eventually become a generational thing, as my own children learned to love those back scratches.

As a teenager I was not known for making good, responsible decisions. I became one of those teenage statistics for pregnancy. My Katie was born and there was an instant connection between Katie and Judy. Oh my, how Judy loved Katie. Her eyes literally sparkled when she talked about Katie, and just to watch the two of them together was remarkable. Judy saw to it that my girls, Katie and Maggie, never wanted for anything. Without Judy I know that I could not be the person I am today. Dad would just smile when he saw Judy around those girls. Never once did he resent the time devoted to being "grandmother," nor did he try to curb her shopping on their behalf (lol).

After I married, we moved away because of my husband's military assignments. It was while on those assignments that Maggie had been born. For two years we were assigned to the Naval Air Station in Fort Worth, Texas. Trains, Planes and Automobiles is name of an old movie, and that became Judy and Dad's mantra. Nothing was going to separate them from seeing my girls and me. During the Christmas season the UPS delivery trucks made daily stops at our house. I later learned that the UPS workers at the shipping facility in Chattanooga had not only learned Judy's name, but when she walked in their door they already knew where those packages were headed.

We finally made our way back to Chattanooga and Judy was always there for us. I began a career, which later led to being able to own my own business. Judy was right there, helping me provide and care for my children. Transportation to preschool, and later school. Sick-day sitter or pick them up when they got sick. Soccer practice, just name it, whatever it was, grandmother was there.

I will always remember the day Dad told me his fears about Judy's memory issues had been confirmed. Judy had dementia. We were all blessed that for a good many years Judy's decline into the world of Alzheimer's moved somewhat slowly. She was still able to enjoy time with the grandkids. Even after her abilities were diminished Dad continued to keep her involved – vacations, football games, church, whatever came along – Judy was by his side. He saw to it that she was treated like a queen. Nails, hair, makeup, how she dressed and so much more – he was determined Judy would remain a constant presence in our lives for as long as possible.

His heart attack became the precursor for some changes and difficult decisions. I could hear and see Dad's brokenness when the time arrived for Judy to move into a memory care facility. There were some major bumps in that process, but he persevered and never wavered. Judy was priority number one.

The final year of her sweet life was hard to watch. She became frail and was losing weight. Eating and drinking became more difficult.

Even then, music seemed to grab her attention, and her foot would bounce to the sound.

Some of my sadness is around the fact that my children did not really have grandmother for several years, even before her death. She was there, but not there. Judy had a capacity to love, and express that love, in a way that one would never question or doubt that love. From the beginning she and Dad had a relationship that was the expression of that deeply, divine love. She shared that love with my daughters and me. I can truly say that Judy not only changed my Dad's life, she changed my life as well. I miss you and love you sweet Judy.

Jennifer Johnston Odister

Chattanooga, TN

I was very young when Grandmother was diagnosed with Alzheimer's, but there are certainly things that I remember. We had an upstairs playroom in Granddaddy and Grandmother's house, and she would take me in that room and help me pull out every toy that I wanted to play with for that day. And she never made me pick up the toys and put them away. I am certain that after I went back to my parents' house that she put every single toy back in its place so that I would know where to find it the next time. I was all into riding "stick" horses at that time and she made me a stable of several stick horses and she allowed me to ride those horses all over the house and the yard. At that time Grandmother and Granddaddy lived on a golf course, right along the first fairway. I remember her taking me to Junior Golf Camp, along with trips to the swimming pool— and of course, snacks from the pool cabana. She also kept my favorite snacks in the house, and she would prepare my favorite foods. Christmas was always a wonderful time with Grandmother— it was always gifts galore for all of us grandkids. Long after she no longer knew us, I can still see her in my mind, as Granddaddy always made sure she was gathered around the Christmas tree, along with all the rest of us.

Alex Clemons

Chattanooga, TN

There are so many fond memories I have of Grandmother. There were trips to Alabama football games during the fall months, and lots of great summer fun with her at the swimming pool. In reflection, every moment that I spent with her is something I both miss and cherish. To be sure there was nothing I wanted for as long as Grandmother was around. She made sure that all the grandkids had everything they needed...and wanted. She had the kindest soul of any person I have ever known. As well as her kind soul, she gave the best back rubs of any person on the earth. After Katie and I would have spent a long day with her at the pool, we would climb up into her king size bed and fight over which of us would get the first turn for one of her fabulous, soothing back rubs. She always sang to us as she would rub our back, and I have no doubt that we would fall asleep every time. Grandmother loved music, and she could certainly sing. Even now, I cannot hear an Elvis Presley song without thinking about Grandmother.

Grandmother always had an adventure for us, and after running around all day I remember that she basically had to force me to take a shower. Getting out of the shower I would always be freezing, and Grandmother would let me use her hairdryer to warm myself up— and, without fail—we would always sing and dance in the bathroom while getting dressed. I remember thinking that she had one of the biggest closets that I had ever seen, and I hoped that one day I could have a big closet just like hers. Many times, after a busy day and showers were done, we would sit on the back porch—eating great snacks—and watch golfers play along the fairway. Grandmother never failed to have a stash of my favorite candy hidden away in the pantry. Gosh, I miss those long, wonderful summer days with

Grandmother, but I am so grateful that I got to make all those wonderful memories.

Maggie Ward

Atlanta, GA

I had little or no understanding what it meant when, at about age twelve, I was told that Grandmother had Alzheimer's Disease. But with each passing year of those fifteen years, I learned the harsh realities of that disease as it took more and more of my Grandmother from me. I can tell you that my mourning for her began long, long before she actually passed away. Having said that, I can also say that I was not ready to say goodbye went the end came. I will forever remember Grandmother's smile. A smile that stretched so wide it could have bridged the ocean. A smile that was so infectious that you just had to smile too. I will always remember Grandmother's love for all her family—and her ever ready willingness to be there for her family, especially her grandchildren.

As an infant and a young child, I spent many days and nights with Grandmother and Granddaddy. If I awoke in the middle of the night, Grandmother was always immediately up with me. I can remember so many times when I would wake up in the night and tell her that I was hungry. The two of us would quickly be off to the kitchen and she would cook me macaroni and green beans—my favorite meal as a little child. Then just as quickly as she had eagerly jumped out of bed with me, she would wrap me up in her arms, scratch my back, and sing me back to sleep—this time with a full tummy. At the "drop of a hat" she would come rushing to school to rescue me from a tummy-ache, and she somehow always knew the cure. We would grab smoothies, get mani-pedi's and top it off with "lite" shopping at the mall. Grandmother's laugh was something to be remembered. Her smile and her laugh were trademarks by which so many readily identified with her.

Grandmother always made certain that I knew how much she loved my Granddaddy. I cannot even begin to count the number of times she would point across the room and say, "Do you see him? That's my man." She even told me once, "when you grow up and fall in love, don't settle for anyone who loves you less than your Granddaddy loves me."

Grandmother was and always will be one of the greatest joys in life —one of the sweetest, most precious parts of my heart. My memories of Grandmother will live on, and my intent is to share those wonderful memories of her with my children and grandchildren.

My sweet grandmother is free from the grasp of that awful disease, and I will miss her all of my days—and just as she said to me hundreds, if not thousands of times—I say to her, "I love you a bushel and a peck."

Caitlin (Katie) Johnston

Chattanooga, TN

The very first time I met Aunt Judy I was around twelve years old, and I wore both braces and glasses. I will never forget that she looked right into my eyes, and with that big smile of hers, said, "Hi beautiful." I certainly did not feel beautiful at that age, but Judy had a way of lifting you up and helping you to gain a sense of who you really are, and how to see yourself in so many wonderful, positive ways.

I also remember watching her make homemade biscuits. It all seemed so effortless for her and I was amazed to watch her use a glass to "cut" the biscuits. At a young age that impressed me, and I remember thinking, "how fancy."

The very last conversation I had with Aunt Judy was around the time I was going through a divorce. She was struggling with her words, but she was determined to talk to me. She knew how unhappy I was, and she recognized my pain, and made sure I understood her thoughts and her heart. What an impression that left with me—there she was struggling with that disease—but now she was doing everything she could to encourage me to be strong and confident in my difficult circumstances. What a memory!

Amanda Dunagan Duke

Prattville, AL

Aunt Judy was beautiful, intelligent, and full of life. Her smile could light up any room, and her voice when singing could make all worries disappear. Her energy level was high, and she was always on the move, no more so than while on the dance floor. Aunt Judy never met a stranger, and I remember how easily she made connections with people. I guess you could say that she was "Facebook" before Facebook was invented. She was a remarkably selfless woman who was so encouraging, and always put others first. I remember going through a really awkward phase as a teenager, and Aunt Judy would say, "Jonathan, you are the most handsome boy in the world." I knew better, but it was great to hear that. Every time our family would gather Aunt Judy would sit down beside me and want to know what was going on in my world.

As the years passed and miles separated us, seeing her courage and perseverance through the "long goodbye" that comes with Alzheimer's was not easy to watch. But it's the memories—her smile, the singing, and all those encouraging conversations—that will always be the Aunt Judy I know.

Jonathan Dunagan

Gardendale, AL

As kids, living on Camp Jordan Road in Chattanooga, was the best time of Judy's and my life. She was a few younger than me, and the baby of the family. I can say with certainty that she was Daddy's little girl, and in his eyes, she could do no wrong. Be sure, Judy knew where she stood with Daddy, and as has been said, she "played him like a fiddle." She always knew how to get Daddy's agreement on about anything. Judy was a skinny little kid, but oh my, those eyes. Black, shiny eyes that could melt any heart. It did not take her long to figure out how to use those eyes to her advantage and she pretty much "ruled the roost." I was the self-appointed protector of my little sister, and I have been known to use my fist to defend her honor. It was always the eyes! I have to admit that as much as I was her protector, I have been accused of having been the antagonist in those early years. One such story that persisted in our family, for decades, was that I once took her bicycle and sold it. But Judy always found a way to get even, and one of her favorite ways of doing that was at the dinner table. Our parents always had a big garden, and Mother loved hot peppers, so they were always grown in the garden. I must be a really slow learner, because over and over I fell for Judy's trick with those peppers. She would take a big bite of a pepper, and then without so much as a flinch, she would offer me one and say, "Roy, these are mild, these are the kind you like." I fell for that line so many times. I would take a big bite and immediately go into orbit from the heat, yelling, screaming and even crying. Judy and Daddy would be rolling with laughter. Again, I fell for that so many times. Again, it was those eyes.

Judy loved to dance, and oh my, she was incredibly good. Maybe it all got started with a Hula Hoop contest at East Ridge Junior High School. Judy was determined to win that contest, and she did! She kept swinging her hips and kept that Hula Hoop swinging for several hours. The teachers had to finally make her stop and, needless to say, Judy won the contest.

In the early 70's, when we were both single, Judy and I both lived in Atlanta. A friend introduced us to a club that had dancing and a live band almost every night. It was not long before Judy had garnered an audience, and a lot of admirers. People would form a circle around the dance floor just to watch Judy dance.

Years later Judy and I both got our lives moving in a healthier direction, and Jesus Christ became the central person in both our lives. Judy's life forever changed when into her life rode her "knight in shining armor." That knight's name was Alan Johnston. Those two were "love struck" and the passion of their love never flickered. Alan not only provided Judy with love, but he also loved my mother and for so many years became the protector and provider, not only for Judy, but for Mother as well. Alan was instrumental in changing my life. On September 2, 1991 Alan led me to a saving knowledge of Jesus Christ. The next week he drove to Douglasville, Georgia and baptized me at my church.

Judy grew up to be such a beautiful woman, not only physically, but spiritually as well. She touched so many lives through her witness, her singing and a never-ending faith in God, no matter the circumstances. And, oh yes, those beautiful, shining black eyes.

You no longer suffer my sweet little sister, and I will see you soon!

Roy Abercrombie

Villa Rica, GA

I was sort of stuck in the middle of our family pecking order. I had two older sisters and a younger brother, and a younger sister. Judy was my "baby" sister by ten years, and then my brother Roy was five years younger than me. As might be imagined, Roy and Judy were often my assignment. Some assignment, huh?

At the time Judy was born my parents owned a small country store, which also had gas pumps out front. It was located on U.S. Highway 41 at the very point where Tennessee and Georgia intersected. This was long before Interstate roadways existed, which meant that all travel between Chattanooga and Atlanta passed right in front of that little store. Roy and I loved playing in the yard with our toy cars and trucks. We would build make-believe roadways and provided all the sounds necessary to make our play time realistic. Our family actually lived in a house that was attached to the store, and next door lived our aunt and uncle. By the time Judy was five or six months old she would join us outdoors by being placed in an oak "Adirondack" chair. Again, my job was to ensure that Judy was okay while Roy and I played in the yard. One day my Aunt Vera, next door, had been visited by her sister, and when her sister went to leave for her own home, she put her car in reverse and she backed over the chair which contained baby Judy. In horror I watched as the car turned the chair over, throwing Judy on the ground. The car continued to back up and would have crushed Judy had not that old oak chair been there to protect her. The car backed up and onto the chair to the extent that the chair lifted the rear wheel of the car off the ground, and that chair was sturdy enough to support the weight of the car. That chair saved Judy's life. That was nothing short of a miracle of God. I certainly did not, at age ten, grasp all the theological ramifications of that incident. But as the years passed and I reflected on that day, it became perfectly clear that God had his hand and heart on Judy's life.

I have never met an Abercrombie that did not think they could sing, and we are a singing family. But this I know for sure—Judy could sing! She had the sweetest alto voice, and she had the gift of being able to blend her voice with the other harmony parts. At every family gathering the five of us (Mary, Helen, me, Roy, Judy) would sing. Gospel songs were always special to us. Songs like *Precious Memories, He Touched Me* and *Amazing Grace* were always among those that we sang. Long after Alzheimer's had invaded Judy's mind, she retained the ability to sing. Along with a Southern Gospel pianist, Roy, Judy and I, got together with the sound engineer at Abbas House in Hixson, TN. The three of us sang eight gospel songs. Our intention was to perhaps get that recording produced and into the hands of the Alzheimer's Association to use to promote awareness of the disease, and hopefully even use as a fund raiser for research to end the disease. That dream is still alive.

We all had a great surprise on the day of Judy's funeral service. The media ministry of Abbas House had retrieved from their archives that recording session. On two giant video screens, during that service, there were the three of us, singing those gospel songs.

Through all the years I never had a better cheerleader than Judy. She always gave me encouragement and loved me unconditionally. I relish the reunion and homecoming celebrations that awaits when I see her once again.

David Abercrombie

Chattanooga, TN

FRIENDS

I have so many fond memories of Judy, before and during her time with Alzheimer's Disease. In the days when we were affiliated with American Express Financial Advisors, we attended many conferences. While our husbands attended meetings, she and I lingered over many lunches. Being the Southern lady that she was, Judy drank lots of sweet tea, and oh how she loved those "Arnold Palmer's" We spent many afternoons sitting by the swimming pool, just talking about our lives, and of course, our families. We shared many tears and a whole lot of laughter through the years.

Now, anyone who knows Judy knows she loved shopping, and we spent many afternoons shopping together. We tried on lots of clothes, and always looked at jewelry. I remember on a trip to Palm Springs that Judy greatly admired a beautiful emerald ring. We couldn't wait to show it to Dave and Alan. Judy was both excited and tearful when Alan bought it for her.

I remember spending a day with her in Chattanooga when she told me she could no longer remember how to write a check, and she was having difficulty telling time. In fact, she was having trouble with numbers in general. This was the first time she made me aware of her recurring problems with her memory.

Because I lived in Nashville, I did not get to visit Judy as often as I would have liked. We had a shared love of music, both sacred and secular, and it would be music that would continue to be our bond long after she had lost other faculties. We also loved to dance to the "oldies" which was great fun! When she was no longer able to read or turn the page in a book, Judy could still sing. We used to sit in her kitchen and sing along with CD's. It amazed me that she harmonized so well.

On yet another occasion Judy and I were sitting on her backyard patio. Words were very difficult for her, which meant that she was not actually able to talk in sentences. Yet, she would begin humming old hymns and they seemed to bring comfort to her. I know this for sure, Judy's humming brought comfort to me! Judy would try to apologize for constantly singing, to which I replied, "Judy, don't ever apologize for that! You are doing what we should all be doing everyday—singing praises to God!" I always went to see Judy with the intention of lifting her spirits; instead it was always Judy who lifted my spirits.

I was thankful for all the trips we made together. Once such vacation was a trip to St. Thomas. Our husbands had gone golfing and I was in Judy's room to help her, if she needed it, so that we could go sit by the swimming pool. She was struggling with her sunglasses. She told me that Alzheimer's caused her to do a lot of strange things, one of which caused her to try to put things on upside down. That of course, was early enough in the diagnosis that she knew what was happening to her.

Alzheimer's eventually took the life of my dear friend and extinguished her bright light on this earth. But her light shining brightly in heaven, where she is, I am sure, singing with the angels.

Sherie Hockenbery

Nashville, TN

When I think of Judy, I think of a huge smile and an infectious giggle. Her whole face lit up when she would laugh. That is the thing I remember most about sweet Judy. I remember her kindness to me and her words of encouragement that always boosted my spirit. But my favorite "Judy story" is about the night several couples from church were invited over to Judy and Alan's house for dinner. I don't remember all the details, but all of we guests had arrived and been there for some time when Judy came bouncing in carrying sacks of groceries. It was obvious that we had not only been invited to eat, but also invited to help prepare the food. And that big smile never left her face and that giggle continued throughout the evening. She just took everything in stride and provided a wonderful meal and many, many laughs. Judy was always a joy to be around. I used to love to go into the Blimpie Sub shop she owned and visit with her. She was, indeed, a very special lady.

Fred Guilbert

(former) Worship Pastor

Central Baptist Church (Abbas House)

Hixson, TN

As I think of my friend Judy, I will always think of music. She loved to sing, and she was a real talent. Alan always made sure that Judy's birthdays were celebrated, and my husband Ben and I were invited to those parties. Before the evening was over, Judy, sometimes along with her brothers and sisters, would be singing. Even after Alzheimer's disease began to advance, she could remember the words to the songs that had so long been a part of her life.

Judy and I also sang in our church choir, and we were both in the alto section. It was, in fact, through our shared experiences in the choir that we became such good friends. Judy and Alan were married about the same time that Ben and I married, which meant we met in the choir shortly after we all joined the church. Our choir seating assignments often positioned us next to each other. She and I made many out of town choir trips together, and since we resided in the same part of the city, we often rode together to and from rehearsals.

Judy continued her participation in the choir even as Alzheimer's seemed to take more and more Judy away from us. Our mutual friend, Edith Kennedy, would assist Judy in getting from our Sunday School classroom to the choir room, and as Judy's abilities continued to decline, I joined Edith in helping Judy. Even though the disease took more and more of her memory, she never lost her love for music. People marveled that long after she could no longer read the notes or the words, Judy never missed a word, nor did she ever miss a note. Judy loved every moment of being in the choir, and we all loved her being in the choir with us. Judy blessed all of us, not only with her musical talents, but with that big, beautiful smile, which just seemed to say, "I love you!"

Oh, by the way – she loved to dance too!

Pat Holcomb

Chattanooga, TN

Alan asked me to share a memory of Judy Abercrombie Johnston, and of course, I said yes! Judy and I spent a lot of time together in our younger years. She was so beautiful, both inside and outside. She had a lovely singing voice, loved to talk, and was witty. She had a sweet spirit and she loved her family and God fiercely.

Judy had the most beautiful brown eyes I have ever seen...they were liquid brown and there was always a twinkle in her eyes and a smile on her face....as though she was up to some mischief.

Judy and I used to spend a lot of Saturdays on my boat, and we always had a lot of fun. However, she always had her makeup applied and her hair perfectly fixed even though we were going to the lake to ride in a boat and to lay in the sun. I can remember spending many nights at her house, where she and her Mom lived. I would be up and completely dressed, with makeup, at least thirty minutes before she would begin applying lip liner. Lipstick alone was never enough – the lips, as well as the eyes had to have liner. In reality, Judy did not need any makeup at all to make her more beautiful, for she was beautiful even without the makeup. But Judy never left her house without perfectly applied makeup, beautifully arranged hair and her attire always made her look like she stepped out of a fashion magazine. Judy was always going to "look her best."

Judy was notorious for being late. Not just ten to fifteen minutes late, but thirty minutes to an hour late. I was once having a surprise social gathering at my house, and I told Judy that we all needed to arrive early so that we could surprise the honoree. I gave Judy an arrival time that was thirty minutes earlier than I asked all the other guests to arrive. Well, not only did Judy not arrive in advance of the other guests, she did not arrive along with the other guests either. In fact, she arrived an hour after the guest of honor had arrived. One of the guests told Judy what time they all arrived, and what time the honoree arrived, and Judy looked at me with a quizzical eye and said, "but you told me to get here thirty minutes earlier than all the guests?" I could only look at my sweet friend and say, "even that plan did not work…you were more than an hour later getting here than anyone else." That may be the only time I ever saw Judy speechless. But it was so funny that Judy, along with everyone else could only laugh about it.

Then Judy met this man, and all of her family and friends knew this was the "one" that had captured her heart! The twinkle in her eye became much brighter when this man, Alan Johnston, arrived in her life. I had never seen her so joyous as she was with Alan, and he gave her so much happiness and love. Their marriage was truly ordained by God and He blessed them both with an enduring love as evidenced by their dedication to each other, and Alan's care for Judy through the difficult years.

Judy was a dear friend that I have missed for a long time now, even before the physical passing of her body to heaven. Over the course of years, that wretched Alzheimer's took the sparkle out of Judy's beautiful brown eyes. But I am certain that she is celebrating seeing her family members in heaven, and I am equally certain that she is gabbing away, telling stories again.

I loved my friend so much!

Sandy Skipper Koss

Signal Mountain, TN

I remember Judy as someone with a lightning-quick wit and sense of humor. She was truly hilarious and almost always had a smile on her face and a song in her heart. When the choir music would start, she was always the first one to stand up and move and dance. Her spirit was contagious to those around her. As a choir director I always wished for 100 more members just like Judy. When I first came to the church, she was one of the first ones to welcome me and she always encouraged me saying, "God brought you here! Lead on!"

I also remember how this awful disease began to take Judy's memory and abilities a few years after I arrived. I remember the heartbreak of breaking down and crying in choir rehearsal when she could no longer read the words on the page, but I also remember her determination and faithfulness in being there and singing regardless. She set the bar for faithfulness very high for all of us.

I will always remember all of those Alzheimer's Memory Walks, which for many years, our choir attended, and we all marched and sang alongside Judy. It was not unusual for "Team Judy" to have 80 to 100 people joining she and Alan in the fund-raising efforts. For many years "Team Judy" won the first-place trophy. She seemed pleased that all of us were there, and the look on her face was priceless.

One of the most memorable times in choir was one of the last times Judy was able to attend. She wasn't there to sing with us—that ability had seemingly slipped away—she just wanted to be with us. Everyone in attendance was cheering and hugging her. Two of our choir members walked over to her and began to sing "Amazing Grace." One man sang tenor while the other sang the melody. Without any hesitation, Judy joined them and began singing flawlessly the alto line in the hymn. It was perfectly on key and she did not miss a word. Her mind had been devastated by Alzheimer's, but her spirit was indefatigable. I learned that day that true worship

159

does not come from the mind, it comes from a place that that disease could not reach. It comes from a person's spirit in communion with God. It was a lesson I will never forget.

All of us still love and miss Judy. I will personally remember her lessons and pass them along to others every chance that I get.

Ken Hartley

Executive Pastor of Ministries

Abba's House

Hixson, TN

Years ago, I was a recently divorced mother of three, and I met Judy while dating her brother Roy. Judy, along with other members of the Abercrombie family became dear friends of mine and I loved them dearly. Life happens, and Roy and I stopped dating, but Judy and I continued our friendship. Judy became more to me than a friend, she became more like a sister.

Throughout the years we maintained that relationship. I visited her often in Chattanooga and she would drive to Atlanta to visit my family and me. My children loved Judy, and she was there with us for so many celebrations, graduations, and other wonderful occasions. Judy had such a positive outlook on life, and a bubbly personality.

After her move to Chattanooga she would come back to Atlanta for weekend visits. Often, we just sat by the swimming pool and spent hours talking about life and faith. And I remember when she met Alan and I knew she had found the great love of her life. It was the match she had prayed and waited for, and I was thrilled for her, because I knew she deserved to be in a happy marriage.

With the passing of years, we remained in touch, even if by distance, but I will never forget Judy's kind spirit, and I will be forever grateful she was a part of my family.

Peggy Green

Atlanta, GA

Judy was always the bright spot in any room. Her smile lit up her entire face. She was always impeccably dressed, whether at a work function, or at home. You just knew how important it was to her to look nice. After the Alzheimer's disease began to take its toll in her life, Alan continued to ensure that she was always dressed to the nines, her nails manicured, her hair styled, and her make-up applied.

Alan and I worked together for many years, and much of the time I spent around Judy was as a couple with my wife and me, or at business functions and parties. I remember that at some of the business conferences she could get a little ornery, if not in fact, bored and eager to get out the door. Sometimes she would lean over and make comments about something or someone relative to the program. Most of the time I had to contain myself from bursting out laughing at her remarks. She would crack me up when I least expected it. Judy was always fun to be around, and it was always obvious that she loved to get all dressed up and dancing the night away.

I can certainly say, there was never any doubt about Judy's love for and devotion to Alan.

Dave Hockenbery

Group Vice President (Retired)

Ameriprise Financial

Nashville, TN

There is a song by Michael W. Smith that begins, "friends are friends forever if the Lord's the Lord of them." I quoted that song at Judy's funeral. Our faith in Christ was truly our bond. She was my friend before Alzheimer's, and she was my friend after the onset of Alzheimer's.

My husband Ron and I met Judy through Alan. He set up a blind double date so we could meet. She and I became instant friends. Judy was so real, so happy, and so funny. Ron thought she was perfect for Alan. We became even better friends after the two of them married. I cannot encapsulate our friendship in just one memory. We spent many weekends together in Tuscaloosa while attending Alabama football games. Our friendship blossomed on those late-night drives back to Chattanooga. We were more like sisters. We talked nonstop about everything. She was a talker, and so am I. It was, at a much later date, on one of those late drives home that Judy and Alan told us about her Alzheimer's diagnosis.

Judy and I modeled together each year for the Bethel Spring Ladies event. What fun! We were young and skinny back then.

Judy and I prayed about many things. We prayed earnestly about how she could be a mother to Alan's girls. She had never been a mother, but less the proverbial stepmom. God answered that prayer by giving Judy such love for those girls, and to this day Judy has a very special place in their hearts. When Katie came along Judy was suddenly in grandmother bliss. My, how she loved Katie—and Maggie and Alex, who came along some years later.

As I said, Judy and I prayed a lot together, and I know how much she loved Alan, and I also remember her praying for Alan that he might know even more of God, and to be filled with the Holy Spirit. Well…you guessed it. Alan had been out of town on business but made it back in on the final night of a Bible conference we were having at church. That evening Judy, and the entire church, saw God move mightily and Alan had a holy encounter with God. Yes, another answered prayer that she and I witnessed.

I remember going to an Alabama football game with Alan and Judy in their motorhome. During the early evening Ron had twisted off the bathroom faucet and the water had to be turned off to the motorhome for the night. Judy and I slept in the master bedroom, and Ron slept on the sofa-bed while Alan slept on a "drop-down" bed. Well, during the night we needed to use the restroom, but there was no water. With flashlights we tiptoed through the motorhome, giggling all the while, and went outside to the porta-toilets set up at the campsite. Everything, it seems, is funny in the middle of the night. By the way, the guys did get the plumbing fixed the next morning.

My last great memory of Judy was at a Christmas party with Alan's Sunday School class at Abbas House. Ron and I sat with Alan and Judy, and by this time Judy had lost a lot of weight, nor could she speak or feed herself. When we sat down Judy moved her face very close to my face and smiled the biggest smile. She did that for the entire evening. It was not the vacant, questioning look of, "I ought to know you." It was more like the look of a little child when his mother comes into the room and picks him up. I knew that somewhere deep inside Judy knew me and was delighted to see me. It was the look of a loving friend. Friends are friends forever....

Paulette Phillips

Abbas House

Hixson, TN

As a preacher's kid I have many memories of romping around the church sanctuary after Sunday services, especially the evening services. It was a safe place, and the members were always ready to give me some attention and tell me how cute I was. Among those always there was Judy Johnston. I have great recollections of Judy sitting on a church pew, with my head in her lap as she rubbed and scratched my back – a little slice of heaven for any kid. She and Alan were friends of my parents which allowed me to have interactions with Judy outside the confines of the church. She always had a way of making me feel special.

Eventually I became a pastor on our church staff, alongside my Dad, and I witnessed firsthand the long battle that Judy endured with Alzheimer's. She did it with great faith and a whole lot of grace. She loved to sing and she, well into her battle, remained so faithful to the church music ministry. The love she and Alan had for each other is embedded in the memory of our entire congregation.

I was privileged to be one of the ministers who spoke at Judy's memorial service. It was truly a celebration of a life well lived.

Ronnie Phillips, Jr.

Senior Pastor – Abbas House

Chattanooga, TN

14

GRANDMOTHER

BY: KATIE JOHNSTON

This account of my grandmother turned out to be a lot more difficult than I originally imagined. I have so many memories of her that I could fill an entire book myself, but to try and reduce a lifetime of love to a few pages felt futile. I am certain that not even the greatest of poets or storytellers could capture her or my love for her in a way that I would feel suitable.

When I was writing my first draft of this, I had decided that I was not going to write about my grandmother's disease. Instead, I was only going to focus on my memories of her before she got sick because I wanted you to know who she was then. Like some poor attempt at a Hail Mary to not let the woman she once was be forgotten. But I quickly realized that I would be doing you, myself, and my Grandmother a disservice. Because while Alzheimer's did not define my Grandmother, it was a part of her story and I fully intend to honor that part too. Living in an ableist world, we often lose sight of the fact that someone's value doesn't depreciate just because their mind or body doesn't perform up to society's standards. My grandmother was an incredible woman before she got sick and she remained an incredible woman throughout her battle with Alzheimer's. Of course, there were many changes—

changes in her moods, changes in her behavior, changes in her abilities...even though things looked different, to me, she always remained.

I got to spend a lot of time with my grandparents growing up, as most children of young mothers do. From the start, me and my Grandmother were quite literally inseparable; I was her favorite person, and she was mine. Even up through middle school I would go over to their house on Saturdays while my mother worked. Grandmother would be up bright and early waiting for my arrival, ready to make cheese toast and pile up on the couch for Saturday morning cartoons and back scratches before we'd go to the pool. If she scratched my back for 10 minutes, she scratched by back for 10,000 hours, which coincidentally is how long scientists say it takes someone to master a craft – and I can assure you, she was a master back scratcher. We'd go on afternoon car rides up and down the hills in the neighborhood pretending it was a rollercoaster, she'd take me to play golf, tennis, ride go-carts – you name it. She was the most fun person I've ever known.

My grandmother wanted me to be a well-rounded person and she made sure of it. Not only did she singlehandedly make sure that I was able to take advantage of every opportunity that came my way, but she would create opportunities for me. She would take me to nice restaurants and give me real-time lessons on etiquette and table manners. We'd get all dressed up and go see plays at the Memorial Auditorium in downtown Chattanooga—"Annie" being one of our favorites. She would constantly be weaving in lessons on how to be respectful and how to become respectable. But one of the greatest lessons I ever learned from watching her was to be kind and gracious to everyone I meet. She would tell me, "You never know what someone else has been through; that's why it's important to be kind to everyone. Even just a smile can change someone's day." She lived by that and I don't think you would find one person that ever-crossed paths with her that wouldn't back up my claim. Joy just seemed to spill out of her.

To say that my grandmother was influential in my life is almost not enough. She taught me how to tie my shoes, potty-trained me, taught me how to sing, introduced me to Elvis, taught me how to be confident in myself and how to be strong and steadfast in the face of adversity. I owe a lot to her. To some extent, I even owe her the credit of my career path. Now, I'm not a CEO or some hot shot in a high rise. In fact, I'm quite the opposite; I'm the operator of my family's small farm in rural Georgia.

Food had always played a huge role in my life and I have my grandparents to thank for that. For a while, I was a "macaroni and cheese" kind of kid, but my grandmother quickly put that to rest. She got the idea one day to give me one dollar for every new food I would try. This might sound like bribery and you wouldn't be wrong in thinking that, but nonetheless it worked. I would try everything and soon enough she didn't have to pay me to try things anymore. Nowadays, my job is to be a purveyor and grower of the finest and tastiest foods around. Trying new foods and exploring flavors from different cultures has become a lifelong love and obsession. A love and obsession that I attribute to her and her dedication to watering my seeds of youth.

I was around twelve years old when she was diagnosed with Alzheimer's. I remember it all began with whispers. My mother started having these long phone conversations that me and my younger sister were not privy to. She would move from room to room, night after night, wherever she could find a corner of the house to talk without one of us hearing. Whispering. My other grandparents would talk in quiet, hushing each other as I would enter a room. I knew something was going on and that no one wanted me to know about it. Finally, I mustered up the courage one day and said to them, "I know something is up. Are you going to tell me what's going on or not?" Nanny looked at me with a sadness in her eyes and said, "No one wanted to tell you yet because we didn't want you to be upset but your grandmother has been diagnosed with Alzheimer's." I was shocked. Alzheimer's? Wasn't that something that old people got? Did that mean she was just going to

167

start forgetting things every now and then? I had no idea what we were up against, but the cat was out of the bag.

A few days later, my grandmother confronted me about it herself on a drive back from my school to her house. She said, "I guess you know that I have Alzheimer's." I nodded yes. "I know it's hard to understand but do you remember when you were little, and I used to take care of you? I would bathe you and feed you and change your diapers. Now, you're going to have to do that for me," she told me. With tears streaming down my face, I said, "I will always take care of you, Grandmother." She took my hand in hers and squeezed it.

I would be many years down the road until I had to do those things but that was the first glimpse that I had of our new reality. I felt unprepared, not just physically but emotionally. I'm not sure you can ever be prepared for something like that, even if you have time to get used to the idea. As much as someone could complain in a situation like we'd found ourselves in, I never heard her complain once. I never heard her question, "why me?" I never saw her be angry at God. How strong of a woman to be able to face such a terrible disease with such composure. Nevertheless, she sailed fearlessly into the storm.

As a teenager, I would go stay with her while Grandaddy worked. We would watch television and drink Arnold Palmer's by what seemed like the gallon. When she got too sick to drive, I'd take her down to get her hair and nails done at my mother's salon on Saturdays. If you knew my grandmother, you know she was always "done up." Her hair was always perfect, she had bright red glossy nails, not a touch of make-up out of place, adorned with the finest jewelry and clothes and truly emanated what I thought the ultimate woman was. Even when she didn't know what she looked like anymore, my Grandaddy would make sure she was able to have her hair and nails done. He truly treated her like the queen that she was until the very end.

Alzheimer's is a tricky disease with a lot of unknowns. Sometimes it happens fast, sometimes it's slow. Some days you feel like you're making progress only to slide right back down the hill and land on your face. In our case, it was a slow and long road with a lot of detours along the way. My grandmother lived for nearly 15 years with Alzheimer's and only a couple of years before she died did things really start to decline. I'll never forget the last time I heard her say, "I love you" to me. I was living in California at the time and unable to attend her birthday party, so the family called me on a video chat. We were talking about what was going on and exchanging our "miss you's" and love you's." When we were getting ready to hang up I said, "Happy birthday, Grandmother. I love you!" All of a sudden, she lifted her head and said, "And I love you." I couldn't believe it; I hadn't heard her speak in sentences in what seemed like years. I bawled that night. That may seem small but that was a big moment to me – to know that somehow, she was indeed still there. And not only had she not forgotten who I was, she still remembered the love that we shared. A love that was and is the most precious love in my life.

I eventually ended up moving back to Tennessee and I'm really grateful that I did. I would have missed out on so many memories with her and other family members that are no longer with us today. Even though our fun looked a little different than it did before, it never slowed us down. We would "boogie" to oldies on her radio, she'd laugh her roaring laugh as I'd pretend to be the Kissy Monster coming for her cheeks, and she'd even get a kick out of it when I'd do "the airplane" while feeding her. This may seem more sad than fun and honestly, I would cry the whole ride home after visiting her, but these are some of my most cherished moments. I was proud to sit with her, to feed her, to sing to her and dance with her. I was proud to get the chance to keep my promise I made to her on that car ride home when I was just a kid.

The next few years were really hard to watch. Sentences that had become mumbled words soon turned to silence, she could no longer focus her eyes or feed herself. But every time I would walk into her room and announce that I was there, she would lift her head, smile that big ole smile and look around for me. I really don't think she ever stopped knowing who I was and my heart overflows knowing that.

The end came what seemed so suddenly. I was in South Carolina on vacation when my mom called me. I knew in her voice the moment I answered that something was terribly wrong. She said she didn't want me to get upset but that the doctors said Grandmother was unresponsive and probably didn't have too much more time. Was this really it? The doctors had said this before, but she'd always proved them wrong. One day she'd be unresponsive and then the next she'd be alert. I didn't want to believe it was true.

My mother and I continued in talks throughout the day and night and I decided that I would leave the next morning and head back to Chattanooga. The news the next morning was worse than the day before. "It's down to hours," my mother said. I frantically packed the car and headed out. That drive was the longest drive of my life. I was literally racing against time to get back to her just one last time. To hold her hand, to sing to her, to tell her how much I loved her, to just be in her presence.

When I finally got to the assisted living facility, I ran into her room to find her in bed and my Grandaddy, faithfully sitting watch by her side. I collapsed in the chair beside her, weeping over her. I took her hand in mine, kissing it and rubbing it. "I love you a bushel and a peck and a hug around the neck," I said. At that moment, I felt her gently squeeze my hand. My heart felt like it was going to jump out of my mouth. She had been completely unresponsive but somehow, she knew I was there. She knew what I was saying, and I believe that was her way of saying, "And I love you," one last time. A true testament to the fact that love has the ability to stretch far beyond what we believe to be possible.

I sat and held her hand by her bedside until close to 1:00 A.M. the next morning. I sang to her, played Kissy Monster, and assured her that it was okay to let go. Even though I knew in my heart that I would never be ready to say goodbye. My grandaddy finally said it was time that we got some rest, and I could come back tomorrow. I knew when I was leaving that would be the last time, I saw her. I stayed with my mother that night in her guest bedroom to avoid having to drive an extra half hour home. Sleeping was the last thing on my mind, but my body finally shut itself off. I woke up early the next morning with an overwhelming sense of peace and I knew in my gut that she had left this world. I laid there, not moving an inch, staring at the clouds outside the window. Sure enough, about 20 minutes later my mother came into the bedroom with tears in her eyes and shaking her head. Her battle, our battle, was over. And just as our favorite hymn promised—she finally got to exchange that old, rugged cross for a crown.

My grandmother was and always will be one of my most favorite people in this world: the most precious part of my heart. She was beautiful, bright-spirited, kind, resilient, gentle, and a fierce lover of her family and of Jesus. I will carry on her memory with me for all my days. She may be gone but she's not out of reach. Sometimes I feel like I can even summon her back to me through music. I'll turn on

Roy Orbison or Elvis and just like that, she's right there beside me— ready to boogie. I imagine her now cruising across the sunbeams in her midnight blue Trans-Am, Elvis on the radio, T-tops down and her hair blowing in the wind, with a smile that permeates the heavens.

Until we meet again one day on the great cosmic highway – I'll be seeing you in all the old familiar places, my sweet Grandmother. I love you a bushel and a peck.

(Written by Katie Johnston, Chattanooga, TN)

15

JOY COMES IN THE MORNING

The calendar had just flipped over into the new year, 1971. Gasoline was thirty-five cents per gallon, our nation was still at war, the stock market (DJIA) hovered just under 900 points, and Disco music would make its way onto the scene. I was still a ministerial student at the University of Mobile and I had just become the pastor of a small-town church in Coffeeville, Alabama. Shortly into our new adventure we discovered that we were expecting our first child, and to say it was exciting is a gross understatement. That was long before ultrasounds were used to reveal the gender of an unborn child, so, as was typical of expectant parents we began to have fun considering possible names. And to ensure we covered all the bases we were trying to settle on a potential name for a boy or a girl. My wife's medical history had raised some concerns about the pregnancy, but we were nonetheless excited. As the months went by the doctor began to express some concerns relative to both the mother and the baby. The baby was due in October, and by September the doctor had become even more concerned and was having us in his office multiple times during the weeks. We seemed to leave each visit with a new list of things to worry about. As concerns grew, and complications were compounding, and the safety of mother and child had become a grave concern. Everyone, including the doctor, agreed that it was going to best for the delivery to take place in a larger, better equipped hospital. We agreed on the Baptist Hospital in Montgomery, Alabama because it was prepared for any eventuality, and it was near my parents' home. After hours and hours of difficult labor, on October 10, our baby girl arrived into a world that had so many unresolved issues. None of that mattered—all that mattered was that little baby girl. Even though, six weeks later, she would require surgery, she seemed healthy, and she was the most beautiful thing I had ever seen. Out of all the names we had considered for a girl, we chose Joy. We chose that name based on a Psalm that we had read again and again. *"...weeping may tarry for the night, but joy comes with the morning."* (Psalm 30:5 ESV) It seemed the most appropriate given the difficulty and fears of the past nine months, and it certainly spoke to the pure joy of holding that precious little baby in my arms. Yes, the night had been long and fearful, but now Joy was here, and my joy was soaring.

I smile every time I read Psalm 30:5 from the Message Bible, *"...the nights of crying your eyes out give way to days of laughter."* Wow! We have all had nights like that, right? Nothing is working, answers aren't coming, circumstances have turned against us, friends have forsaken us, life is not working out like we thought it would. That particular phrase from Psalm 30:5 is even more impactful when read it in context with the entire verse, *"All you saints! Sing your hearts out to God! Thank him to his face! He gets angry occasionally, but across a lifetime there is only love...."*

This Psalm of David comes with a somewhat dark, and at times, foreboding backdrop. There had been times when David had to go into hiding, for there were those who sought to kill him. He had experienced betrayal, even from his own children. He had also allowed himself to move far away from God, doing as we humans often do, deciding to do what we want to do, regardless of the consequences. In Psalm 51 David reached a low point, cried out to

God, asking that God would help him to find joy once again. Like David, I know what it feels like to have the joy knocked out of your life. Without joy life can feel bleak, empty, and hopeless. I have expressed how those dark moments often crept into my life during Judy's long illness and death. But no matter the length of the night, the blackness of the darkness, there eventually comes the morning – and with it the promise of light and joy.

Paul, in the New Testament book of Philippians, adds rich and meaningful context to the depth of the joy that belongs to any Christian. Paul certainly had his share of adversity. He had friends who had forsaken him. He became an outcast to the religion of his youth. He had a lingering disability. He was often called on to settle squabbles and quarrels among church members. He had once been lost at sea because of a shipwreck. He had been jailed numerous times. He was on the "most wanted" list of religious fanatics. He had been the victim of an attempted murder. Yet here he is in this letter to the Christians in Philippi, writing to them about the joy that was his. In this short letter he uses the word rejoice or joy fourteen times. If anyone, from a human perspective, had a reason to lose his joy it was Paul, but no, he is still writing and preaching about the joy that cannot be lost. What can be made of this remarkable fact?

In Philippians 3 there are three basic truths about the joy we all seek. The Apostle begins by saying, *"rejoice in the Lord,"* and moves quickly to remind the reader that there are enemies of joy that stand in our path. From the perspective of our faith Paul provides us with a list of that which can rob us of our joy. He begins verse two by saying, *"Look out for...,"* or as the KJV says, *"beware."* To use a bit of alliteration he warns us about defilers, deceivers, and distorters. The defilers are those, like King David, who live on with unconfessed sin hanging over their head. In Psalm 32 David recounts what unconfessed sin can do to a person's character and psyche. He added to that, in Psalm 51, his mournful, repentant plea that he might have his joy restored. A life lived counter to God's Biblical principles and standards will be a life void of real joy. He also alludes to a group that I have referred to as deceivers and distorters.

Paul saw them as those individuals who are false teachers, including those who add to the singular message of grace that the gospel of Christ proclaims.

In the third verse Paul turns his attention to the expression of joy. Paul makes certain that we know that in Christ we have a new identity. In the previous verse he blistered those (the Judaizers) who taught that grace alone was not enough for salvation. They taught that physical circumcision was also a requirement of salvation. Paul repudiated that, and so must we. We still find ourselves trying to add to the simple gospel of saved by grace. What, you might ask, could that be? Many believe they must earn salvation by way of doing something...whether it be good works, baptism, or even speaking in tongues. The gospel that brings lasting joy is the gospel of God's grace plus nothing. But here (v. 3) Paul alludes to *"the circumcision who worship by the Spirit of God."* Paul elaborates greatly on this subject in Galatians by stating, "For all who rely on works...are under a curse..." Thankfully, he goes on to say, *"Christ redeemed us from the curse...."* His reference to circumcision in verse three is a reference to our heart, to our spirit. We have a new identity in Christ. The old has passed away, and we are made completely new (2 Corinthians 5:17). What joy! Paul also states that our expression of joy is exercised through us *"by the Spirit of God."* The Apostle Peter says it this way, *"...you believe in him and rejoice with joy that is inexpressible and filled with glory."* Again, what joy! Paul goes one step further when he says, *"and put no confidence in the flesh."* I take that to mean that in Christ I have a new independence, that is, I don't have to live according to the whims or wiles of the flesh (any action taken without regard for God). Through the presence of the Holy Spirit within us we are fully armed to defend ourselves from thoughts and actions that will rob us of our joy in Christ. Independence means freedom, and we are free from that old curse. Let's say it one more time – What joy!

Finally, in verses four through eight, Paul gives us an example of joy and provides an illustration to help us understand the concept of joy. For Paul it was a matter of simple math. He added up everything that he was and had in his life. He was highly educated, he had a profitable career, he was held in high esteem in his religion, and he came from a highly regarded family. Of all that and more, he said it is a total loss, it is like rubbish when compared to knowing Jesus Christ as Lord. In other words, Paul's joy was not derived from that long list of stuff, rather, we see it in his statement, *"…that I might know him and the power of his resurrection…."*

So, like Paul, we must look outside ourselves and our circumstances for joy. Our moods are often changed by circumstances. I can be happy one moment, then sad the next. But the joy that comes in the morning, the joy that comes after the long, dark night, is a joy without limits or constraints. It is joy full of glory.

It is now been almost three years since Judy passed on to paradise. Not a day passes that I am not reminded in some way of her and the life we had. But those remembrances are not as painful as they once were. The things I did following her death I did simply because they had to be done, it was expected of me. But there was little joy in anything I did. Theologically I know that the joy I have was never gone, but it was clouded over by my grief. Now that joy has begun to return, or as King David would have called it, restored.

I have discovered that for me the renewal of joy has come about because of several things. Perhaps one of the most rewarding thing has been around relationships. Twice in my life I have walked through those dark shadows that David talked about in the twenty third Psalm. Each time I did something that was destructive, detrimental, to my recovery. I withdrew from people, from relationships. I allowed myself to get trapped in my own world, my thoughts, my perceptions of how things are or would be. As has been said, I was just going through the motions. I readily confess that the restoration of joy has come largely through relationships. God has used other people to fill my life with hope and purpose. My family, my church family, new friends, and acquaintances that God has brought into my life. Key among those relationships is Dowdy. She is a beautiful woman whose heart is more God centered than any person I have ever known. Her walk with God is both impressive and inspiring. She and her husband were members of the Bible study class I have taught for many years. He had a long battle with cancer and when he passed away, I conducted his funeral service. Professionally she was an elementary school teacher who later went back to graduate school for a degree in counseling, and for more than a decade was a faith-based counselor. She is a gifted Bible teacher and began the original women's ministry in our church. After Judy's death I mustered the courage to ask her to dinner and a movie. Dowdy has helped me rediscover joy, and what a joy when I asked her to marry me…and she said yes! God is good —all the time. She has been God's fulfillment for me of Isaiah 61:3, *"…to grant to them a beautiful headdress instead of ashes, the oil of gladness instead of mourning, the garment of praise instead of a faint spirit."* What joy!

The thought of a reunion is also a great joy. Like many people my age I have so many loved ones who have passed on from this life. I have enjoyed working on my ancestry, and as might be expected, it has created moments of nostalgia and fond memories of family no longer visible to me, yet I know they are still very much alive. Their spirit lives on in that place Jesus called paradise. The Bible promises us that they are not lost to us, only temporarily separated from us, and one day soon we will see them again. I have learned to chase away the occasional moments of despair with the wonderful thoughts of what an old gospel song called *"That Glad Reunion Day."* What joy!

Finally, what great joy I find in the realization that there lies ahead an event called the resurrection. Jesus lives! Evidence bears witness to that fact. Paul said, *"If in Christ we have hope in this life only, we are of all people most to be pitied."* Bill and Gloria Gaither wrote and made popular the song, *"Because He Lives."* The chorus to that song says this:

> Because He lives I can face tomorrow,
> Because He lives, all fear is gone,
> Because I know He holds the future,

And life is worth the living, just because He lives.

In 1 Corinthians Paul is contemplating the love of God when he says, *"For I am sure that neither death nor life…nor anything else in all creation will be able to separate us from the love of God in Christ Jesus our Lord."*

What joy!

ABOUT THE AUTHOR

Though a native of Alabama, Alan has lived in Chattanooga,

Tennessee for more than forty years. He grew up in the rural community of Elmore, near Wetumpka, Alabama. Following graduation from Wetumpka High School he moved to Birmingham, Alabama to begin his educational and career pursuits.

He is both an ordained minister and a Certified Financial Planner (CFP©). His ministry now spans more than fifty years, and he has more than thirty -five years of experience as a financial planner. He has served as Senior Pastor of churches in Alabama and Tennessee and was a founding partner of Oracle Wealth Management (a branch of Ameriprise Financial) in Chattanooga, Tennessee. For the past 35 years Alan has also served as a Teaching Pastor for Abba's House (Central Baptist Church) in Chattanooga.

Alan is also the founder and leader of Path2truth Ministry. He continues to preach and teach and some of that ministry is available on the ministry website as well as Youtube. Paththh2truth has as its mission "to teach and preach the good news of Jesus Christ – in so doing, to bring Christians into a fresh encounter with God, to equip and encourage the church to be authentic, and to empower believers to share God's redemptive message."

Alan earned his BA degree from the University of Mobile and additionally holds five advanced degrees and three professional certifications. Those degrees and certifications cover such disciplines as History, Theology, Counseling, Finance and Conflict Management. His educational pursuits spanned Samford University, the University of Mobile, Luther Rice Seminary, UT-Chattanooga, The American College and The University of Alabama.

Alan is an avid reader and writer, and is as well, an avid fan of college football and basketball. As time permits, he enjoys playing golf.

Most important of all….Alan is a husband to Dowdy, a father to Joy and Jennifer and "G"-daddy to grandchildren Katie, Maggie, Alex and Benjamin.

Made in the USA
Middletown, DE
19 January 2022